CHRISTIAN SOLDIERS

CHRISTIAN SOLDIERS
THE DISCIPLINE OF HOLY LIVING

WINSTON ABRAMS

authorHOUSE®

AuthorHouse™ LLC
1663 Liberty Drive
Bloomington, IN 47403
www.authorhouse.com
Phone: 1-800-839-8640

© 2009, 2014 Winston Abrams. All rights reserved.

No part of this book may be reproduced, stored in
a retrieval system, or transmitted by any means
without the written permission of the author.

Published by AuthorHouse   08/01/2014

ISBN: 978-1-4389-5694-7 (sc)
ISBN: 978-1-4670-5598-7 (e)

Any people depicted in stock imagery provided by Thinkstock are models,
and such images are being used for illustrative purposes only.
Certain stock imagery © Thinkstock.

This book is printed on acid-free paper.

Because of the dynamic nature of the Internet, any web addresses or
links contained in this book may have changed since publication and
may no longer be valid. The views expressed in this work are solely those
of the author and do not necessarily reflect the views of the publisher,
and the publisher hereby disclaims any responsibility for them.

Table Of Contents

Part – A
<u>Creation</u> – The Rise And Fall Of Man
From Innocence, Into The Army Of Satan...................1
    Chapter #1 Disobedience Of Man And The Entrance Of Sin
                        Sin's Penalty, Sin's Power And Sin's Presence...3
    Chapter #2 Sin – The Enemy Of All Mankind.....8
    Chapter #3 The Holiness Of God – Our Mission And The Goal Of All Believers Is To Become Christ-Like.........................17

Part – B
<u>Salvation</u> – Good News For Man
(Into The Army Of God) The War Begins.................25
    Chapter #1 Obedience Of The God-Man Christ Jesus And Salvation From Sin..........27

Part – C
<u>Sanctification</u> – The Transformation Into The New Man – The Battle Rages On 35
    Chapter #1 Enlisting In The Army Of The Lord – The Battle Strategy (Training Or Discipline) 37
    Chapter #2 Discipline Of A Soldier....................42
    Chapter #3 Discipline Of Athletes
                        A Runner's Discipline......................49

Chapter #4	Discipline Of Athletes – A Body Builder's Discipline	56
Chapter #5	Discipline Of Believers Prayer And Fasting	58
Chapter #6	Discipline Of Believers Bible Study, Meditation And Scripture Memorization.	67
Chapter #7	Discipline Of Believers Spirit Filled	72
Chapter #8	The Discipline Of Believers Renewing The Mind, And Having The Mind Of Christ	83
Chapter #9	Discipline Of Believers – Eternal Vigilance	101
Chapter #10	Discipline Of Believers – Fellowship	112
Chapter #11	Discipline Of Believers – Separation From The World	121
Chapter #12	Discipline Of Believers – Stewardship	127
Chapter #13	Discipline Of Believers – Silence, Solitude And Reflection	139
Chapter #14	Discipline Of Believers – Training Of The Lord - To Build Your Faith Or Break Your Will.	144

Chapter #15 Discipline Of Believers Mortifying "Killing" The Flesh 162
Chapter #16 Discipline Of Believers Motivation For Doing Right (The Love Of God) 168
Chapter #17 Duty Of Believers – Obedience 174
Chapter #18 The Ultimate Discipline The Cross 184

Part – D
<u>Glorification</u> – Transformation To Perfection
Army Of The Lord Victorious 187
    Chapter #1   Fate Of Satan And Fallen Angels ... 189
    Chapter #2   Fate Of Non-Believers 191
    Chapter #3   Fate Of Believers 193

Preface/Introduction

I have to thank the Lord for making this book possible. I am simply a weak, feeble, sometimes disobedient, but willing servant, who loves the master. I am not only thankful for His grace and mercy, but I can truly thank Him for showing me that He truly loves me and that I am His child, by not leaving me to myself and not letting me have my own way. Also, thanks to Pastor Jerry Johnson, a man used greatly by God, for his assistance in proofreading and guiding me, and the invaluable contributions and corrections he has made to the manuscript. He and His wife, Sister Scharmel Johnson's love, dedication and service to the master are a continuing source of inspiration and encouragement to me, and I am sure, countless others. If you have truly met the master – the commander in chief, our Lord Jesus Christ – you will love Him, and you will have a burning desire to please Him. Even more so as you apprehend the truth as stated in scriptures, "we love Him because He first loved us". If this book helps but one person, it will have been worth the time and effort and served its purpose. For if there was but one person that needed salvation, Christ would have gone to Calvary's cross for that one person, with the same commitment, purpose and self-sacrifice with which he has for a world of hell-deserving, wicked sinners such as you and me – so great is His love for every one of His creation. Ironically, the writing of this book is another paradox of the master's ways to ponder: The master has chosen the "chiefest" of sinners – me, to write a book on holiness. His ways are truly above our ways!

PART – A

CREATION – The Rise and Fall of Man From Innocence, Into the Army of Satan

Chapter #1

Disobedience of Man and the Entrance of Sin
Sin's Penalty, Sin's Power and Sin's Presence

In the Bible, in the books of Isaiah and Revelation, we are told that Lucifer, the anointed cherub, was created to worship God in heaven. God created him very beautiful, and more than likely, well endowed to perform his area of service. The scripture says Iniquity was found in him. He became puffed up with pride and self delusion because of his beauty (Ezekiel 28:15-18). We are later told that Lucifer began a war in heaven, and one third of the angels fought with him against God and the other angels. Lucifer and these angels were cast down to the earth (Revelations 12: 4-9), where they are now known as Satan (Devil, Deceiver), and fallen angels (Demons). The Lake of Fire was created and will be the eventual end of Satan and these fallen angels (Revelation 19:10).

In the book of Genesis we are told, "In the beginning God created the heavens and the earth" (Genesis 1:1). We are later told that God created man in His image and placed him in the Garden of Eden with the explicit command to eat of every fruit, except the fruit of the tree of the knowledge of good and evil (Genesis 2:15-18). We can see from scriptures that Adam and Eve had personal, intimate, unbroken fellowship with God. Lucifer, now the fallen angel Satan, disguised himself in the form of a serpent and deceived Eve into disobeying God by causing her to eat of the fruit she was instructed not to eat (Genesis 3:1-5). We are given a glimpse of Satan's character in this initial act of deception, perpetrated by the wicked one, on mankind. Later on in scriptures, we see that Satan is called a counterfeiter. II Corinthians 11:13 says, "… for such are false apostles, deceitful workers, transforming themselves into the apostles of Christ. And no marvel; for Satan himself is transformed into an angel of light."

It is not stated in scriptures why Satan chose to use the serpent as his instrument of deception. We do know that he is described as being cunning, among other things. We also see that Eve was in the garden, prior to her encounter with the wicked one, obviously observing the forbidden tree every day. But, it was not until the devil pointed it out, that she came to the realization of the tree's potential. Genesis 3:6 says, "And when the woman saw that the tree was good for food, and that it was pleasant to the eyes, and a tree to be desired to make one wise, she took of the fruit thereof, and did eat…" The remainder of the story

– which is probably the most universally acknowledged fact of history – tells us that Adam and Eve ate of the forbidden fruit, thereby bringing damnation on all of mankind. As we all know, the remainder of the story is history, as the saying goes. God cursed man, woman, the earth, Satan – literally all of creation (Genesis 3:6-22).

This single act of disobedience is the tragedy that brought the entrance and penalty of sin upon all mankind. Romans 5:12 says, "Wherefore, as by one man sin entered into the world, and death by sin; and so death passed upon all men, for that all have sinned". God told Adam and Eve that the minute they ate of the forbidden tree "they would surely die". Satan told them that "they would become like gods". The consequences of this act of disobedience have been passed down to every single human born through the lineage of Adam and Eve, literally all of mankind. The minute they disobeyed God, they died spiritually. That fellowship they enjoyed with God was broken. They began to die physically and will die eternally in the Lake of Fire, without intervention. We see that God made provision for Adam and Eve's disobedience by providing a covering. Genesis 3:21 states: "Unto Adam also and to his wife did the Lord God make coats of skins, and clothed them." This covering was a type of Christ's atoning sacrifice – blood was shed. The scripture says, "... And without the shedding of blood there is no remission" (Hebrews 9:22).

The scripture also says, "The disobedience of one man brought death to all men". So, we see that man, the creation of God, began life in innocence, with freedom to worship the creator. But, due to disobedience, he was translated from the kingdom of innocence into the kingdom of sin and darkness. At this stage man is under the condemnation and penalty of sin and on his way to eternal damnation in hell – the Lake of Fire. Hell, or the Lake of Fire, was originally created for Satan and his fallen angels, but as the scripture says in Isaiah 5:14, it had to be enlarged: "Therefore hell hath enlarged herself, and opened her mouth without measure; and their glory, and their multitude, and their pomp, and he that rejoiceth, shall descend into it." Hell had to be literally enlarged to accommodate all of mankind who dies without trusting Christ as savior. The following article, from an unknown author, illustrates the condition of fallen man:

"The Recall Notice"

"The maker of all human beings is recalling all units manufactured, regardless of make or year, due to a serious defect in the primary and central component of the heart. This is due to a mal-function in the original prototype units code named Adam and Eve, resulting in the reproduction of the same defect in all subsequent units. This defect has been technically termed "Subsequent Internal Non-Morality" or, more commonly, known as S.I.N., as it is primarily expressed. Some other symptoms include: Loss of Direction, Foul Vocal Emissions, Amnesia of Origin, Lack of Peace and Joy, Selfish or Violent Behavior, Depression or Confusion in the Mental Component,

Fearfulness, Idolatry and Rebellion. The manufacturer, who is neither liable nor at fault for this defect, is providing factory-authorized repair and service free of charge to correct this SIN defect. The Repair Technician, Jesus, has most generously offered to bear the entire burden of the staggering cost of these repairs. There is no additional fee required. The number to call for repair in all areas is: P-R-A-Y-E-R. Once connected, please upload your burden of SIN through the REPENTANCE procedure. Next, download ATONEMENT for the Repair Technician, Jesus, into the heart component. No matter how big or small the SIN defect is, Jesus will replace it with: Love, Joy, Peace, Patience, Kindness, Goodness, Faithfulness, Gentleness and Self-Control. Please see the operating manual, the B.I.B.L.E. (Believer's Instructions Before Leaving Earth), for further details on the use of these fixes. WARNING: Continuing to operate the human being unit without correction voids any manufacture warranties, exposing the unit to dangers and problems too numerous to list, and will result in the unit being permanently impounded. DANGER: The human being units not responding to this recall will have to be scrapped in the furnace. The SIN defect will not be permitted to enter Heaven, so as to prevent contamination of that facility. Thank you for your attention! GOD.

Please assist where possible by notifying others of this important recall notice, and you may contact the Father any time by "KNEE mail".

Chapter #2

Sin – The Enemy of All Mankind

What is sin? Sin is defined as missing the mark. Anything short of God's Holiness is absolute sin. 1 John 3:4 states: "sin is a transgression of the law". Leprosy, in the Old Testament, was a type of sin, the incurable disease of the soul. Sin is an act of breaking the law or commandment of God. Sin is a state – the fallen state of man without righteousness. Sin is the nature of fallen man at enmity against God. The following specific sins are mentioned in the Bible:

- ***Exodus 20:3-17, I***: Idolatry, cursing, Sabbath breaking, disrespect to parents, murder, adultery, stealing, lying and covetousness.
- **1st Corinthians 6:9-10**: Effeminate, masturbation, drunkards, revilers, and extortionist.
- **Romans 1:29-31:** Unrighteousness, fornication, wickedness, maliciousness, envy, debate, malignity, whisperers, backbiters, haters of God, despiteful, proud, boasters, inventors of evil,

covenant breakers, without natural affection, implacable, unmerciful.
- **1st Timothy 1:9-11:** Lawlessness, disobedience, ungodliness, profanity, whoremonger, kidnappings.
- **Colossians 3:5-8**: Inordinate affections, evil concupiscence, anger, wrath, malice, blasphemy, filthy communications.
- **Galatians 5:19-21**: Lasciviousness, witchcraft, hatred, variance, emulations, strife, seditions, heresies, retellings.
- **Mark 7:20-23:** Evil thoughts, an evil eye, foolishness.

Jesus said if you look at a woman with lust, you've committed adultery in your heart. He also says if you are angry at your brother without cause, you are guilty of murder. We are told that God sees the heart and judges the very motives. Disobedience is "not conforming to God's Word", and all disobedience is sin. James 2:10 tells us that if we kept 99% of the law, but stumble in one point, we have violated them all, for the commandments are a whole. We are told in Isaiah: "all our righteousness is as filthy rags", and "the heart is deceitful and desperately wicked". In the book of Genesis we are told: "Man's every imagination is only evil continually", (Genesis 6:5). We are given ten (10) commandments in Deuteronomy 5:7-21, and the seven abominations of God in the book of Proverbs (Proverbs 6:16-19). In the New Testament, 21 categories of sin are listed, with a total of 202 individual sins; of which 103 are distinctly different. A careful study of individual sins listed in the Bible reveals that inner sins of the heart are listed alongside outward actions of the flesh, with no distinction. There are no little sins and big sins. Sin is sin in the eyes of an absolutely Holy God. Lust, anger, irritation, annoyance, resentment, frustration, anxiety, worry, doubt, hopelessness and discouragement, are all sins, as indicated in scripture.

Definitions of sin:

- **Transgression** – Psalm 51:1, the overstepping of the law.
- **Iniquity** – An act inherently wrong as breaking a commandment.
- **Error** – Psalm 51:9, the departure from right.
- **Missing the Mark** – Romans 3:23, 1 John 5:17, failure to meet divine standards.
- **Trespass** – The intrusion of the self-will into the sphere of God's authority.
- **Lawlessness** – 1st Timothy 1:19, Spiritual anarchy.
- **Debt** – James 4:17, a failure in duty, omission, things left undone.
- **Unbelief** – Hebrews 3:12, an insult to the divine prerogatives of God. Quite simply, sin cannot be hidden from an all seeing God.

Numbers 32:23 tells us: "Your sins will find you out." **Proverbs 28:13** also reminds us: "He that covereth his sins shall not prosper". God sees and uncovers hidden sins.

Adam, Cain, Achan, Ananias and Sapphira, these all tried to hide sins from the LORD, but failed in their efforts.

The Results of sin:

- **Death – Romans 6:23. Lost – Luke 15:24.**
- **Condemnation – John 3:18.**
- **Guilt – Genesis 26:10.**
- **Perdition – 1st Timothy 6:9.**
- **Punishment – Matthew 25:46.**
- **Eternal Fire – Jude 7.**
- **Hell – Matthew 25:41.**
- **The Lake of Fire – Revelation 20:14.**

1 Peter 2:2 gives us a list of internal sins, sins of the heart. Very simply the Bible says: "What is not of faith is sin." The only remedy for sin is JESUS CHRIST. He has defeated sin and death for us because we simply could not. The disease of all mankind is sin, and the only cure for this disease of the soul is Jesus Christ's blood and righteousness. In the world today, mankind seeks to eradicate the disease of sin by dealing with its symptoms. This will never work. One author sums it beautifully when he says, "The heart of the human condition is the condition of the human heart." We need to deal with the cause, the human heart. Only Christ can give a new heart. For, the saying shines through: "God formed us, sin deformed us, but only Christ can transform us." In God's economy, there is Sin and Holiness, not varying degrees. It is not a little Holy or a little sin. Those are man's dichotomy. With God, it is either one or the other.

The word Holy only applies to God – The Father, the Son and the Holy Spirit – and the word sin only applies to man. Our enemy is sin, and the instruments of sin are: Our Self (The Flesh or old man as the Bible calls it), the world and the devil.

We take a light view of sin because, number one: We are too far from a Holy God, and number two: We look at the outward manifestations of this dreaded disease of the soul. We need to look at the heart – our wicked hearts, and the wicked heart of all mankind. What the scripture says will always ring through, "The heart is wicked and deceitful above all things. Who can know it?" We do not see our need to be rescued, or cured, from this dreaded disease, because we do not see sin in its proper perspective. A brother in Christ and I were discussing the state of Christianity today. I mentioned that I felt if someone from the church a century ago arrived on earth today and observed our churches, he or she would probably conclude that most of the people in our churches are not truly saved. My brother's reply was less generous; for he said he believed the conclusion would probably be the church had been raptured out. Such a sad commentary is an indictment on us all that name the name of Christ, in these last days. The church is very subtlety being led, in the guise of "modern times", to accept the things and ways of the world. Sin is relative to us, but absolute to a Holy God.

The church was meant to be the salt of the earth, to check, or keep the world honest in a sense; in more ways than one. If the church kept its ground as the world dived deeper into sin, one look back at the church would have brought conviction to the world. The world is seeking to get God out of the picture because if it acknowledges the fact that there is a creator, it would then have to be responsible to that creator. The world wants to do as it pleases. Just as the time in the Old Testament which states that when there was no king in the land, men did what was right in their own eyes. The Bible states that God has written moral laws on the hearts of mankind. Men know the truth but are seeking to eradicate it, so they can live as they please. One author states it thus, "As time progress, the world goes one-step deeper into sin, and the church takes over where the world left off." In other words, the Church is one step behind the world as it slides, or should I say dives, deeper into sin. Remember, the sin of pride – initiated by Lucifer – is the sin that started it all. If pride was the only sin passed down to, and perpetrated by, Adam and Eve, we would still need a savior to save us from sin and its consequences; for "all disobedience is sin", and Christ would still have had to die on Calvary's cross. We are told in scriptures that we are shaped in iniquity, and we learn iniquity from birth. We are fallen in every aspect: spiritually, morally, mentally, physically – we are totally depraved. Our thoughts, desires, actions, learning – our experience, and most of all, scriptures, confirm it. But though the Bible teaches that man has the capacity to be absolutely sinful, it is clear that our totally depraved nature is not realized to its fullest capacity on a daily basis. The Bible is clear that this is only because of the mercies of God. None of us can ever say, "I would never do that", to any form of evil perpetrated by anyone. The most we can honestly say is, "I hope that, by the grace of God, I never perpetrate such evil."

There is evidence of evil everywhere. Even our so-called "noblest deeds" are tainted with self and pride. Everything is dirty; even our whitest white is dirty gray, our righteousness is truly as filthy rags, in the sight of a Holy God. One author penned, "Our noblest heroes are soiled heroes, all of them. So we learn to excuse and overlook, and not to expect too much. We don't expect all truth from our teachers, and we don't expect faithfulness from our leaders. We quickly forgive when they lie and vote for them again. We don't expect honesty and trustworthiness from anybody, and we manage to get along in the world, not only by passing laws to protect ourselves from the criminal elements in society, but also even to protect us from the best elements in society who might, in a moment of temptation, take advantage of us. Today we are told, "There are no moral absolutes." In other words there is no right or wrong. Whatever makes you happy and feels good, do it. We make excuses by hiding behind adages like, "oh nobody is perfect". Nobody is perfect, but a holy God commands, "Be ye holy, for I am holy." Physically, we wake up in the mornings with our mouths dirty, in need of washing. Why? God in his wisdom is telling us and reminding us of something every morning. Simply,

Christian Soldiers

there is nothing good in us, and nothing good can come out of us. We wake up and have to deal with our dirty mouths. What comes out of the mouth is the evil within our hearts. The Bible says, "From the abundance of the heart the mouth speaks." It is not what goes into a man that defiles him, but what comes out. The reason the world thinks it can please a Holy God by its good works is because it is looking at the outward manifestations – the symptoms – of sin. Symptoms can be stopped. Obedience to laws can be mimicked, but on the inside, the heart, with its wrong motives and impure thoughts, is still in need of cleansing.

Our mission, and by extension, our objective as believer, is to bring honor and glory to God; our Commander-in-Chief, our master; and help spread the good news – the gospel of His salvation. 1st Corinthians 6:20 states, "For ye are bought with a price; therefore glorify God in your body, and in your spirit, which are God's." Jesus not only died to save us from the consequence of sin. If that was the case, He would have taken us home to be with Him in Glory the moment we accepted Christ as savior. He left us in this world to bring honor and glory to Himself by making us new creatures, better individuals, and the salt of the earth. The world will then see our transformed lives and seek to know the source of our transformation. We are left on earth to spread the gospel, with our lives, as much as with our lips. The devil's goal is to get us to fail our mission by sinning. As was intimated above – and we can never be reminded of this fact too much – our enemies are the devil, ourselves (the old nature), and the world. Our adversary the devil is described as a liar, a deceiver, cunning, crafty, and subtle just to name a few.

The reason the world is duped into believing it can work its way to heaven, and work to remain there, is because the world does not have an accurate picture of sin; and most importantly, an accurate picture of the absolute holiness of a Holy God. People do not need better environments, or more programs, to become better individuals. Adam and Eve were in a perfect environment. Don't get me wrong, these things are needed, but the fact remains, and will always be, we need a new heart. Just as Jesus told Nicodemus, "you must be born again."

Chapter #3

The Holiness of God – Our Mission and the Goal of All Believers Is To Become Christ-Like

Romans 8:29 states, "…he also did predestinate us to be conformed to the image of his Son…" Due to my desire to do my master justice, and convey on paper "The Holiness of God", this has been the most difficult chapter to write; for I know that whatever is written here can never do justice to an infinitely holy God. It should be no surprise that the chapter on sin was the easiest chapter to write. As we vaguely apprehend and appreciate the love of God, it will bring us to tears of joy. As we vaguely apprehend and appreciate the holiness of God, it will bring us to tears of sorrow, brokenness and remorse over our sins. One needs to study the Old Testament and see how God dealt with sin (disobedience) before Christ's (God in flesh) virgin birth, sinless life, death and resurrection to apprehend even a glimmer of the holiness of God. All of the aforementioned attributes of Christ had to be true to fulfill the atonement necessary for our salvation. If you take away any one of these truths, there is no atonement, no salvation, and as the apostle Paul says, "we would be of most men most miserable."

Hebrews 9:7-12 says: "But into the second went the high priest alone once every year, not without blood, which he offered for himself, and for the errors of the people: The Holy Ghost this signifying, that the way into the holiest of all was not yet made manifest, while as the first tabernacle was yet standing: Which was a figure for the time then present, in which were offered both gifts and sacrifices, that could not make him that did the service perfect, as pertaining to the conscience; Which stood only in meats and drinks, and divers washings, and carnal ordinances, imposed on them until the time of reformation. But Christ being come an high priest of good things to come, by a greater and more perfect tabernacle, not made with hands, that is to say, not of this building; Neither by the blood of goats and calves, but by his own blood he entered in once into the holy place, having obtained eternal redemption for us." We cannot discuss the holiness of God without describing two of His attributes – Justice and Love. God is absolutely holy. Moses' encounter with God on Mount Sinai gives a glimmer of God's holiness. Exodus 24:15-18 states: "And the Glory of the Lord abode upon Mount Sinai, and the cloud covered it six days and on the seventh day, He called unto Mosses out of the midst of the cloud. And the sight of the glory of the Lord was like devouring fire on the top of the mount in the eyes of the children of Israel."

In the Old Testament, the priest and the children of Israel went through elaborate ceremonies of killing animals and confessing of sins, according to instructions laid down by law. The temple, where most of the sacrifices were done, contained an inner chamber called the Holy of Holies. This was the innermost part of the tent, where God's Glory dwelt. (Exodus 44:4). The high priest was the only one allowed to enter the Holy of Holies – only once a year, and not without blood. He was required to perform the sacrifices and ceremonies precisely, according to strict specifications. The blood from the sacrifices, shed for his sins, and the sins of the entire community, was taken into the Holy of Holies. If the priest did not take blood, the presence of God would instantly strike him dead. The closest few words that any human can use to describe God are: "He is a consuming fire." No one else was allowed to enter the Holy of Holies. Therefore, the priest's robe was designed with bells at the bottom, and a rope was tied to his ankle. As the priest moved and performed his rituals, the bells were heard outside. This allowed those outside to acknowledge that he was still alive. If the sound of the bells stopped, those outside knew that the priest was killed by the presence of God. The rope was then used to pull the priest out of the Holy of Holies. Such is our God – "a consuming fire". Who can stand in His presence but for the sacrifice and perfect righteousness imputed to them by the spotless Lamb of God – Christ Jesus (Revelation 4:1-2)? Glory to the Lamb indeed!

Holy is defined as: Purity, moral excellence, rectitude, honor, truth, and righteousness. God is absolutely Holy, the Holy, infinite one. Mortal language cannot express his Holiness. His Holiness is beyond finite thought, for all of God's attributes are infinite. They are beyond the power of mortals to grasp, or finite words to express. History tells us that the Old Testament writers held the name of God so Holy, and in such reverential awe, that they refused to speak it with their mortal lips. They went through elaborate preparations simply to write the name of God. They thoroughly washed their entire body, spent much time in meditation and introspection, for such was their reverence for the very name of the only, holy one. Compare that to today, where the name of God is taken in vain so much that it has become a common word, almost to the point of becoming derogative. Heaven help us! One author penned it thus: "If God was to tell us how white He is, we would understand only in terms of dingy gray." God speaks of himself as fire, (Habakkuk 12:29, Isaiah 33:14). Who among us could dwell in the presence of the eternal flame?

In the book of Revelation, we notice that the angels do not rest day nor night, but simply bow down before the Lord singing, "Holy, Holy, Holy" as though going through a mechanical, preordained process. One author says, in his opinion, "it is not so much that they are going through an automated process, but more of an automatic process; for when they look up and apprehend the Glory of God, there is no other response that comes naturally, but to bow down again, come up, and repeat those glorious words, Holy, Holy, Holy, for all eternity. Such is His Glory, and majesty. What is this devouring fire? It is the presence of God. We would all melt at God's presence if we beheld Him in all His glory and splendor. The apostle John fell down in Revelation 1:17, "as dead", when he encountered the master in all His glory. Everyone that encountered God in his glory, in scriptures, fell on their faces in remorse and repentance, and in most cases, confessed their sinfulness and unworthiness. In the book of Acts, the apostle Paul was blinded when he encountered the Lord – the God that dwelt in the Shekinah, between the wings of the seraphim – on the road to Damascus. The light that blinded him was the God that dwelt in the burning bush. Moses was told to take off his shoes when he encountered the Lord, for the very ground became "Holy Ground" due to the presence of the God of all creation – "the Holy One of Israel", the one that spoke the entire universe into existence, and upholds everything by His righteous right hand. For in Him we live and breathe and have our being. Today, we come to God dirty and we command and demand of Him, telling Him what He must do, instead of getting down on our faces and begging Him for mercy. If we came to God dirty but trembling and shaken and awestruck in His presence, if we knelt at his feet and cried as Isaiah did in the book of Isaiah (Isaiah 6:5), "I am a man of unclean lips", we would do well. Father, please continue to give us a sense of your holiness so that we will not sin and excuse it, but that repentance will be deep in our hearts. The author, AW Tozer, said of his day, "It was common, when God was the center of human worship, to see people kneel at the altar and shake, tremble, weep and perspire in agony of conviction of their sins, thus begging for forgiveness in true repentance." This was the kind of true repentance King David spoke of when he penned: "Return to me the Joy of your salvation and renew a right spirit within me."

God alone received sacrifices and offerings in the Old Testament. They were to be a sweet smelling savor, as incense to please him. The offender was guilty of sin against a Holy God and was subject to God's wrath. King David said, "Against you alone have I sinned, and done this wicked thing." God had been offended and dishonored, as He is by every sin, committed by every person, who has ever lived. In the Old Testament, God provided a way in which the sinner could come before Him and temporarily have his sin dealt with. The offerer would bring an animal to the priest, in the tabernacle or temple, and lay his hands upon the animal, thereby transferring his guilt (Leviticus 1:1-4). The animal was killed because God requires death for sin. The blood of the sacrificed animal was poured upon the altar, and the person was temporarily cleansed. This cleansing was not permanent; therefore the sacrifices had to be repeated, again and again. JESUS BECAME THAT SACRIFICE TO GOD, FOR SIN – ONCE FOR ALL. In the Gospels;

we see that, in the temple, the veil that separated the Holy of Holies, where God's glory dwelt, was rent – literally torn – in two, when Christ was crucified (Matthew 27:51). This signified that all those that come to God though Christ now have free access to the Holy of Holies of old, or His throne of grace, today. There is no separation or segregation. We that are in Christ, all have equal access to the throne of Grace. As the scripture says, "We can approach the throne of grace boldly." We are all saints and priests. Hallelujah! Glory to the Lamb! The ground is truly level at the foot of the cross.

Jesus' perfect life is credited to the account of all those who accept Christ as savior, thus making the hell-deserving sinners righteous. The imputed robe of righteousness gives wicked, hell-deserving sinners access to the very presence of a Holy God. Nothing added, nothing taken away. Glory to the lamb! Holy, Holy, Holy indeed. Charles Spurgeon in his poem titled, "The Robe" writes: "I will greatly rejoice in the Lord (Isaiah 61:10) – Look upon your past sins, look upon your present infirmities and all your future errors, and while you weep tears of repentance. Let no fear of damnation blanch your cheek, you stand today robed in your Savior's garments…Christ's righteousness is compared to fair white linen, to wrought gold, to the best robe – better than the angels have, I poor prodigal, once clothed in rags, companion to the nobility of the sty, fresh from the husks that swine do eat, am nevertheless clothed in the best robe and so am accepted in the beloved." An unknown author in the poem titled, "A Puritan Prayer" sums it up thus: "Oh God of grace Thou has imputed my sin to my substitute, and has imputed his righteousness to my soul, clothing me with a bridegroom robe, decking me with jewels of holiness. I have no robe to bring to cover my sins, no loom to weave my own righteousness. I am always standing clothed in filthy garments, and by grace am always receiving change of raiment. I am always going into the far county; and always returning home as a prodigal, always saying, Father, forgive me and thou art always bringing for me the best robe. Every morning let me wear it, every evening return in it, go out to the day's work in it, be married in it, be wound in death in it, stand before the great white throne in it, enter heaven in it, shining as the sun."

It is not so much that God hates sin (which He does). The reality is that God is holy. The idea is that the two are mutually exclusive. Just as light and darkness cannot coexist, so sin and holiness cannot coexist, for they are absolutely and infinitely apart and separate. There is no such thing as percentages of holy and perfect – only, holy and perfect. And those two words only apply to God – the self existent one, the Alpha and the Omega – the consuming fire. In the book of Revelation, John looked at the holy one on the throne, and the only earthly description of what he saw and heard was: "Bright shining light, and words as of thunders of lightning." The angels around the throne of God sing Holy, Holy, Holy is the Lamb, and we can sing here on earth: wicked, wicked, wicked is the man.

PART – B

SALVATION –
GOOD NEWS FOR MAN
(INTO THE ARMY OF GOD)
THE WAR BEGINS

Chapter #1

Obedience of the God-Man Christ Jesus and Salvation from Sin

2nd Corinthians 5:19 states: "To wit, that God was in Christ, reconciling the world unto himself…" The scriptures teach that God is Love, but it also teaches that God is holy, and a God of justice. Disobedience always has to be dealt with in God's economy. To satisfy His love, holiness, and justice, God, the creator, the self existent one, came down on this earth in the form of His Son, Jesus Christ, and paid the penalty for the sins of all mankind. In order to save us from the penalty of sin, Christ shed his blood on Calvary's cross. Salvation is very simple and free. It is not cheap; for Christ's blood was shed. Romans 10:9, 10 states: "That if thou shall confess with thy mouth the Lord Jesus, and shalt believe in thine heart that God has raised Him from the dead, thou shall be saved. For with the heart man believeth unto righteousness and with the mouth confession is made unto salvation." Notice! It does not say with thy works performing unto righteousness. It says: "But with the heart believing unto righteousness." All those that accept Christ as savior, instantly appropriate the righteousness of Jesus Christ. The religions of our day teach what one can, and has to do to be saved. The Bible teaches what the true and living God has done to save us – Christ paid it all – for there is nothing we can do, in ourselves, to appease the wrath, and fulfill the righteous requirements of a Holy God. Believe and be saved! Simply believe and be saved!

Man, in his finite wisdom, is being confounded by the wisdom of the all wise, true and living God. The scriptures say, wisdom of God is wiser than man, and is actually considered foolishness to man; for man in his own wisdom seeks to establish his own righteousness. I think that no other story, in the Bible, best illustrates the simplicity of salvation than the story of Naaman, captain of the host of the King of Syria. The captain had leprosy. He, through a series of events, was led to the door of the house of the prophet Elisha. For it was told him, "Would God my Lord were with the prophet that is in Samaria!" "For he would heal him of his leprosy" (II Kings 5:3). The scriptures goes on to say, "And Elisha sent a messenger unto him, saying, Go and wash in the Jordan seven times, and thy flesh shall come again to thee, and thou shalt be clean" (V. 10). The captain was obviously upset for he said: "Behold, I thought, He will surely come out to me, and stand, and call on the name of the Lord his God, and strike his hand over the place, and recover the leprosy. Are not Abana and Phar'par, rivers of Damascus, better than all the waters of Israel? May I not wash in them, and be clean? So he turned and went away in a rage." His servant told him: "My father, if the prophet had bid thee do some great thing wouldest thou not have done it? How much rather then, when he said to thee, Wash, and be clean? Then went he down and dipped himself seven times in Jordan according to the saying of the man of God; and his flesh came again like unto the flesh of a little child, and he was clean." Such is the gift of salvation – for the Lord said, simply believe and be saved! Simply trust! Glory Hallelujah!

Christ shed His blood and died on the cross, satisfying the wrath and righteous requirements of a Holy God. As can be seen from studying the books of Exodus and Leviticus, God's Holiness always demanded that sin be paid for by the shedding of blood, death. The Bible says, "And almost all things are by the law purged with blood; and without shedding of blood is no remission; "For the life of the flesh is in the blood" (Hebrews 9:22). Blood always had to be shed to pay for sins. The animal sacrifices of the Old Testament were simply a temporary covering; they never paid the penalty for sins absolutely; they only covered sins temporarily, and therefore these sacrifices had to be done year after year, after year. Christ became the perfect sacrifice once for all. The Scripture tells us that we are saved by grace through faith, and: "For as by one man's disobedience many were made sinners, so by the obedience of one shall many be made righteous" (Romans 5:19). Not only is it impossible for sinful, mortal man to fulfill the righteous requirements of a Holy God, God in

His infinite wisdom, and knowing man's tendency to take credit for things done by God – which I call the Lucifer syndrome – being proud and boastful as we are, made salvation a free gift or an unmerited favor. He alone can – and rightly so – take credit for salvation, from beginning to end. He alone deserves all the honor and glory and praise. As the scripture says: "Not of works, lest any man should boast. For we are his workmanship, created in Christ Jesus unto good works, which God hath before ordained that we should walk in them" (Ephesians 2:8,9 and 10). God is a jealous God, and He will share His glory with no one; for He alone deserves all glory, and praise, and honor, and worship, and thanks. Glory Hallelujah!

Death, nowhere in the Bible, means to cease to exist. Death simply means to be separated. We were created eternal spirits and souls, in a temporary body. When Adam and Eve disobeyed God they instantly became separated, in fellowship, from God. When we "die" so to speak, our soul and spirit instantly become separated from our bodies, and our flesh goes back to the dust, leaving us to suffer all the consequences of its sinful actions, for all eternity. Those who have trusted Christ as Savior will instantly be in the presence of the Lord. The Apostle Paul said, "to be absent from the body is to be present with the lord". Those that have not trusted Christ as Savior will go to the place of torment and wait to be thrown eternally into the Lake of Fire, with Satan and his fallen angels, to burn for all eternity. All things in the Old Testament pointed to Christ – The Old Testament was a shadow of things to come, the substance being Christ. Christ was the perfect sacrifice once for all. The theologians rightly say: "The Old Testament is New Testament concealed and New Testament is the Old Testament revealed." God has truly revealed Himself to us, in these last days, through His son. He made a way to bring us back to Himself. John 1: 29 states, "Behold the lamb of God which taketh away the sin of the world." Hallelujah, praise His name! If you've never accepted Christ as your Savior, you are still a part of the army of Satan, and on your way to the Lake of Fire. You will spend a Christ-less future there; and you will burn for all eternity. That is the reality, as described in scriptures. The tragedy is no human being has to go to hell, for Christ has paid it all. Just accept what He has done for you. If you've never accepted Christ as Savior, there is nothing stopping you right this moment. The Bible says, "Today is the day of salvation." No one is promised tomorrow.

One author rightly reminds us thus: "It is presumptuous on the part of any human, to assume that he or she has another minute to live on this earth." You can be saved and know that you will go to be with the Lord when you die. In 1st John we are told, "These things are written so that you may know that you have eternal life." Every sin, ever committed, by everyone, throughout human history, can be covered by the blood of Jesus. Simply cry out to God. Tell Him you are a sinner, and that you accept what His Son did on the cross for your sin. The Bible teaches that if you do that, sincerely from the heart, the Lord will save you. Matthew 6:33 tells us: "Seek ye first the kingdom of God and His righteousness." Seek Him today. Tomorrow is not promised.

When one sincerely trusts Christ as Savior, Christ's righteousness is imputed to that individual, *instantly* making that individual righteous in the sight of a holy God. That individual is at this point, "saved" – Saved from the consequences of Adam and Eve's sin – Saved from eternity in the Lake of Fire. Glory Hallelujah! Who the Son sets free, is free indeed. This is what Christ, our Savior, described when He said: "Ye must be born again." At the new birth, the believer is sanctified (to be set apart by God) positionally, instantly, but also begins the practical process of being sanctified, daily. The arduous process of sanctification begins. We see from scripture, when one trusts Christ as savior, one instantly becomes a child of God and gets translated from the kingdom of darkness into the Kingdom of light, instantly leaving the army of Satan, and entering the army of the Lord. The Bible teaches that we are all creations of God, but we are not all children of God. This is the born again experience spoken of by Jesus to Nicodemus. He was told by Jesus that, "you must be born again" – this is not a second or subsequent experience, this happens instantly as a consequence of trusting Christ as Savior. Also, instantly the Holy Spirit takes up residence in your physical body, making your body the temple of the one, true, living and holy God. You have, at this stage, become regenerated – by the birth into new spiritual life, you become alive spiritually. That fellowship with God that was broken by Adam and Eve's disobedience is instantly restored. Salvation begins in a simple confession of faith, and believing in the heart. Nothing added, nothing taken away. The salvation experience must be realized, and appreciated, practically, day by day, by rigorous and arduous discipline. The discipline of practical sanctification – being set apart – begins. The war against the devil, the world and the flesh commences; as the popular adage goes "let the war begin". If you've never trusted Christ as your savior, you are on the other side in this war, and the aforementioned does not apply to you. You must trust Christ as savior first – You must be born again. The Bible teaches that we are all creations of God, but lost the right to be call children of God, when Adam and Eve transgressed; but Glory to God, the scripture goes on to say, "but to as many as receive Him, to them gave He power to become the sons of God, even on them that believe on his name." Glory Hallelujah!

PART – C

SANCTIFICATION –
The Transformation into the new man – THE BATTLE RAGES ON

Chapter #1

Enlisting in the Army of the Lord – The Battle Strategy (TRAINING OR DISCIPLINE)

The army of the Lord is the only army in which one enlists and engages in battle at the same time. A believer is training and fighting at the same. The Christian life begins with a simple confession of faith and belief in the heart (Romans 10:9and10), but it is lived practically by strict discipline – which includes prayer, Bible study, scripture meditation and memorization, sacrifice, service and devotion, and at times solitude (temporary getaways) and silence – in a word, "DISCIPLINE." The Dictionary defines discipline as: "Training, especially training of the mind or character." "The training effect of experience, or misfortune." "A trained condition of order and obedience." "Order among school pupils, soldiers, or members of any group." A particular system of rules for conduct." "Punishment; chastisement to bring to a condition of order and obedience, or bring under control -To Train." Discipline comes from the word disciple. A

Disciple is a believer in the thought and teaching of any leader – a follower. "In the Bible especially, a follower of Jesus Christ, or an adherent who accepts the instruction given to him and makes it his rule of conduct." The most applicable aspect of this definition to the believer, and to the theme of this book is: *Especially training of the mind or character, and a trained condition of order and obedience to the believer.* From looking at the afore listed definitions, we can safely say that to be a true disciple of Christ – which all believers are called to be – we must discipline ourselves to show that "we are truly a believer in the teachings of God's Word, and to truly make it our rule of conduct, thereby bringing Glory to our commander in chief – The Lord Jesus Christ.

My definition of discipline is: "A rigorous, systematic, calculated, ordered, and in some cases, painful set of routines specifically designed to accomplish a goal". It is in this vein the crux of this book is addressed.

King David said, "One thing have I desired, and that will I seek after, to dwell in the house of the Lord and to behold his beauty all the days of my life." Think of desiring one thing so badly, that you set your every waking moment, every action, towards maximizing the possibility of realizing this goal. Your daily routine is structured and designed towards this end. This is what it takes, as a believer, to live as the master, our Commander-in-Chief, would like us to live – sanctified and set apart – He deserves no less. As the title implies, the believer immediately enters a war at conversion. As a consequence of trusting Christ as savior, you are saved instantly and your body becomes the temple of the Holy Spirit, whereby God the Holy Spirit takes up residence in your body. When you turn to Christ you are also transferred from the kingdom of darkness (Colossians 1:13). At conversion, the believer becomes a Christian Soldier, enters the army of the Lord, and immediately enters the war. The believer is thrown into the battle, sometimes, it seems, on the front line. Don't faint, for the scriptures say, "Greater is he that is in you than he that is in the world." Hallelujah! This is unlike a traditional war. Traditionally, a soldier enters an army, and begins the rigorous discipline or training. When he is deemed ready and the need arises, he is sent to the battlefield. A Christian Soldier enlists in the Army of the Lord, by way of trusting Christ as Savior, and immediately enters the rigors of warfare. The Christian soldier is a rookie who needs to be trained or disciplined. The scriptures say to the believer: "Desire the sincere milk of the Word that you may grow thereby." You can say that the Christian Soldier is the only soldier that undergoes training on the battlefield.

In a traditional army, a soldier is first thrust into arduous discipline, with a regimented dose of physical training and mental preparedness. The soldier is also taught how to identify the enemy, and brought to realization early, that his training and preparedness, or lack thereof, is tied to his success and/or survival. He is also taught that his readiness can help to protect the life of his comrades and ultimately determine the outcome of the war. It's interesting to note: the experts tell us that in a traditional athletic competition, the outcome has already been determined, for the best trained and prepared team has already won. They say that the actual match is basically a formality. To whatever degree you agree, it is a very interesting thought. As believers, the choices we make, to a large part, have already been decided by our training and preparedness – our decisions are simply a natural outcome of what we've already purposed in our hearts. We need to learn that life is about choices; and choices have consequences; good choices lead to good consequences, and bad choices result in bad consequences. In order to make the right decisions, we need to spend time with the master – our Commander-in-Chief, the Lord Jesus Christ. We also need to be in training, or strict discipline. The Christian soldier's battle is not physical – it is spiritual. The enemies are: self (the old nature), the world and the devil. The scripture tells us that we wrestle not against flesh and blood. The goal of the enemy is to influence us to sin. The Christian soldier's ultimate goal is to bring glory to the name of Christ. When we sin without repenting continually, the Christian soldier not only fails by dishonoring the master's name (which is the ultimate), but also becomes ineffective in the battle, and eventually is sidelined. We are ambassadors of Christ, and as ambassadors, we represent, or act on behalf of, our Commander-in-Chief – the Lord Jesus Christ. Our conduct is tied to the glory of His person. When we commit sin we sin against God.

Christian Soldiers

A soldier needs to know his enemy. He also needs to identify his strengths and weaknesses and make provision to combat those areas in which he is deficient with extra discipline and training in those areas. We are told in scriptures, "our weapons are not carnal…", and then we are given the spiritual armor to put on. We are then told, "Put on the whole armor of God." In a practical sense, we have the power of prayer to our Father through our Lord and Savior Jesus Christ. We have the Word of God to direct us and cleanse us, and we also have the Spirit of God indwelling us and convicting us of sin and righteousness. In the Scriptures we are told, "…Not by might nor by power, but by my spirit saith the LORD of hosts." Discipline or training is key to the believer living a life that is pleasing to the Lord, and being effective in the spreading of the gospel of His salvation. The Bible tells us that we are given all things that pertain to life and Godliness (2nd Peter 1:3), and that, "All scripture is given by inspiration of God and is profitable…" Now, herein lies the key. We are told, "be not conformed to this world (Romans 12:1), but be transformed by the renewing our minds." Transformed with what? With the Word of God; for the scripture says, "sanctify them through Thy Word for Thy Word is truth."

Chapter #2

Discipline Of A Soldier

The following list chronicles the discipline one must undertake (Basic Training) if desirous of becoming a soldier in the most powerful, physical, army in the world. The following excerpt is taken from the U.S Army Basic training web site.

"BASIC TRAINING"

"Certainly if you have been to basic training you will always remember your first day. As you laid in your bunk on that first night, thoughts were rushing through your head and your mind was scrambling trying to remember everything your Drill Sergeants taught you. Your muscles and mind were fatigued. On that first night, you felt helpless, alone and at the bottom of a very big hill to conquer. For all you recruits who entered the military I will tell you this, your first day will be the worst. You will be homesick, in a new environment and you will not see an end in sight. This will be a time where you need to be mentally tough. You have to remember to take your days one at a time because looking at the entire 9-weeks ahead of you will be very difficult. This takes place after the Reception Process (when all your paperwork and medical tests are completed). A bus or cattle truck will pick you up. You will be packed in a crowded vehicle and you may or may not have Drill Sergeants on board. If there are Drill Sergeants they will either introduce themselves, tell you to be quiet or ask you to sing the star spangled banner as loud as you can. Drill Sergeants look intimidating, but do understand, they cannot physically hit you. Tip: Try your best not to show off or stand out at this point. There is always one person on that ride who tries to show he/she is different."

The Drop-Off

"When the vehicle stops, all the recruits will be asked to get out as fast as they can. At this point, you may be asked to do a number of various exercises. I will use my first day as an example. When I got out of the vehicle they asked 150 other recruits besides myself to line up and place our luggage in a perfectly straight line, in alphabetical order, in under 3 minutes (which is 45-seconds in Drill Sergeant time). Seeing how it is impossible for 150 strangers to know each other's names, we were forced to do exercises because of our failure to complete the mission. You will fail the first mission you are asked to accomplish; it is designed that way. The purpose of basic training is to turn you from a civilian to a soldier in 9 short weeks. In order to do that you need to realize how difficult it is to become a member of the strongest military power in the world. Tip: At this point, you need to show your Drill Sergeants you are capable of handling physical activity. Mentally prepare for physical activity when you wake up in the morning on the day you will meet your Drill Sergeants. Also, don't be letdown when you fail your first mission, which is what the mission is designed for, failure."

Lights Out

"Despite your physical fatigue, you will have trouble sleeping. Your mind will be shuffling through many thoughts. Before you go to bed make sure each member in your sleeping area is prepared for the next day. Often, recruits will need help preparing their uniform or finding certain items. Offer your assistance, your kindness will be appreciated and the favor will be returned in the future. Tip: Keep the big picture in mind and remind yourself why you joined the Army, and how proud everyone will be of you when you return. Mental toughness is 99% of surviving basic training. Recruits arrive at Fort Jackson for general orientation."

"This is where your civilian life becomes part of the Army world—from bidding farewell to family to getting your Army haircut to making sure you're physically fit." "Once Reception Week completes, it's now time to understand new rules, regulations and processes involved in being in the Army. Classroom instruction begins. Leaving the classroom for the field, it's time to test your physical and mental endurance, and also get trained in First Aid and map reading. One thing you'll realize in Week 03 is to believe in the mantra: mind over matter. Physical and mental challenges build as you start simulated combat drills. Learning to shoot a rifle is more than pulling the trigger. Marksmanship courses teach new recruits not only the proper way to hold a weapon, but also how to breathe and stand while firing are equally important.

"This is where the previous weeks' work pays off: tests in endurance and marksmanship await all recruits. Each recruit is only as strong as his platoon. During Week 06, bonds are tested and trust exercises implemented." Hand grenade training; live fire exercises; foot marching; and overall physical fitness are tested in the Confidence Course. It's time to put everything you've learned up to this point to the real test: a three-day field retreat to Victory Forge. All your hard work has led you to this day. Family and friends eagerly await to see you complete your Basic Training course."

"With the Drill Sergeant leading the way, the recruits begin to navigate their way through Basic Training. Moving from the classroom to the field, they encounter physical tests that challenge their bodies and minds."

"After a week of processing through Reception, the recruits are quickly ushered into the Army way of life. In the classroom, on the field and in the barracks they adjust to the new rules, responsibilities and expectations being ingrained deep into their minds."

"The M16A2. It is the standard issue weapon of the U.S. Army, and the recruits' new responsibility, demanding their knowledge and respect. Before a single round can be discharged, numerous nuances like breathing, stance and mechanics are covered meticulously and rehearsed methodically."

"The standard record fire course consists of 40 target exposures at ranges between 50 and 300 meters in timed target sequences and combinations. The objective of qualification is to access and confirm the individual proficiency of individual firers."

The standard course requires 23 hits to qualify as Marksman, 30 for Sharpshooter, and 36 for Expert." As week three begins, the recruits must rely on sheer determination to meet the mounting physical and mental challenges of the simulated combat scenarios.

"The recruits' self-assurance is growing and they are becoming stronger, but that does not guarantee the success of the recruit, the company or the platoon. That success is ensured by the growing bond between the recruits in the field and in the barracks."

"This week, two of the more decisive moments loom in front of the recruits' the Basic Rifle Marksmanship Qualification and the 'Fit to Win' Obstacle Course. Their fortitude, both mental and physical, will be thoroughly tried and tested."

"The Fit to Win Obstacle Course is a valuable physical fitness-training tool. The 900-meter course presents the recruits with challenges to help them develop and test their basic skills. Recruits are required to negotiate and clear up to 20 obstacles while running, jumping, dodging, climbing, traversing, vaulting, balancing and crawling." As the recruits master the various obstacles, they also embody several of the Army Core Values. By overcoming their own physical limitations and supporting other recruits, they develop a deeper sense of personal courage, respect and selfless service. The course includes the following obstacles:

"All the miles have been marched and all the obstacles left behind. The recruits have arrived at Victory Forge, a three-day field outing in which they apply all that they have learned. This is the true and final test of the recruits' skills and spirit' when they prove that they have what it takes to be a U.S. Army Soldier."

"Confidence in themselves, their platoon and the Army way of life has been growing steadily over the past seven weeks. All of this will be proved true as the recruits tackle the Confidence Course this week."

"With their biggest challenge now behind them and graduation just ahead, the recruits finish up some important details before their final day in Basic Training. Family and friends eagerly await this ceremony, as the recruits prepare to join the honorable legacy of those who have served before them."

Having completed the rigorous discipline of basic training, one is now ready to be called a soldier in the United States Army. The difficult part is that, if one does not graduate, the privilege of being in the army is forfeited.

This is not the case in the army of the Lord. The Lord not only provides the method of entrance into His army, He also provides the assurance of entrance, and the certainty of victory. Glory to God in the highest indeed!

Chapter #3

Discipline Of ATHLETES A RUNNER'S DISCIPLINE

From the days of the Roman Empire of old, we have the Olympics, where there are competitions in various disciplines, with prizes awarded to the winners. The athletes must go through strict, regimented discipline, in order to even stand a chance of winning a prize. The apostle Paul compares the Christian life to that of a runner in a race. The following exert, taken from the web site: "Discipline of a Marathon runner", chronicles the discipline a marathon runner undertakes.

"Excerpts From A Marathon Runner"

"I can now run a long, long way without feeling out of breath, but I know physically my legs will feel very tired. I know that I'll get blisters on my feet. I'll find that I'll get soreness throughout my body and my back as well. The training is very difficult and I can understand why people think I'm strange at the moment. Especially as I have to run 5 miles before I come to work, do a whole day working, spend the whole week working and then go for maybe a 2 or even 3 hour run at the weekend. At the moment even I think I'm a little bit mad!'" Six grueling months of sweat and pain come down to one February day for a Texas Tech student. The length of a marathon is 26.2 miles. Perry said she started her training in August by running three miles at a time. She said she now runs up to 16 miles at a time.

"Training for this marathon has been like a lot of little races," she said. "I have set little goals of certain miles." Since day one, Perry has kept a log of her running process. She said she runs every day of the week except Monday and Friday. "I have two days off a week," she said, "and Sunday is my really long run."

Perry said she takes vitamins every day and does not drink caffeine, eat junk food or drink alcohol. "You have to discipline yourself with eating," she said. Not only has training for this marathon taught Perry how to manage her time, but it also has proved to her that running is fun, Perry said. "You hit a mental mark," she said. "You would be surprised what goes through my mind. I run out of music (to listen to). I run out of things to think about."

Ibbetson said runners will learn training information at the workshop, including: setting up a running schedule, different training programs, the right nutrition, proper clothing and the correct running form. "This workshop is being offered to help (runners) prevent injuries and to give (runners) the common procedures," she said. "It's grueling. You need information before you start training."

Ibbetson said getting a person ready for a marathon depends on each person's overall base level of running and exercising. "While one person may be ready after four months of training," she said, "it might take another person more than a year to prepare." "I am seeing food in a completely different way now that Madelyn Fernstrom from 'Today' and Liz Applegate from 'Runner's World' magazine have set me straight on its true purpose: fuel for the body. You need a certain amount of carbs, protein, and fat, in order for your body to function optimally. This is not very different from a car needing oil, fluids, and gas to run smoothly. I don't know why it took me over four decades to understand this, but now that I do, I've changed my eating habits for the better. I am drinking way more water than I ever have, and I am eating fruits, vegetables, and proteins in larger quantities than ever before."

"I don't want to suggest that the story ends there and that my new leaf is permanently glued right side up. The car analogy is working for me at the moment, but I know that there are some powerful emotions tied up in food and this is where the analogy falls apart. None of the cars I've ever owned have gotten emotional about gas and oil. But food for me has been at the heart of many different emotions."

"I almost salivate when I think about the extraordinary coconut cream pie at my favorite restaurant. And I experience comfort, pleasure, satisfaction, and even pride when I eye my gorgeous Thanksgiving meal the moment before my guests begin to devour it. And I can't forget the negative emotions — the revulsion, disgust, and even the pain — I felt during a brief period when bananas caused blisters in my mouth. Negative emotions associated with food can be particularly difficult to forget. When I was 10, I watched a Burt Reynolds movie, while struggling through a stomach virus. To this day, I can't watch that movie without feeling slightly queasy."

"So there are two masters to serve when it comes to food: my body and my brain, or at least the part of my brain driving my emotions. I need to please both to win my battle with food. If I do what is right for my body and tell my brain to stay out of it, it will be very disappointed and most likely direct me to the nearest Dairy Queen in protest. On the other hand, if I give my brain what it desires, I will struggle to eat the right foods — in the right quantities — for my body."

"Of course, this is a battle many of us have to contend with every single day. But for those of us who are long-distance runners, there are additional dietary considerations. We need more complex carbs and lean protein to give us sustained energy during long runs and to help repair our muscles afterwards. You can think of this as a game albeit with some pretty silly rules. My game looks something like this: **There are two beasts to feed:** The brain, which wants what it wants. And the body, which needs carbohydrates to create the energy needed for running. If you give both beasts exactly what they crave, you will be obese and die of heart disease. Here are the rules of the game today (they change frequently): You must maintain a ratio of 50 percent carbs, 25 percent protein and 25 percent fat or you will not run as well as you could, according to Madelyn Fernstrom's book, 'The Runner's Diet: The Ultimate Eating Plan That Will Make Every Runner (and Walker) Leaner, Faster, and Fitter.'

- You must not exceed your maximum caloric intake on any given day. Consequence again is obesity.
- You must keep your sugar intake in check because it's bad for you. (My rule: each person will have one or two). Consequences are cancer, failing memory, and heart disease, if you believe the bad press.
- You must have eight or more glasses of water a day. Consequences are difficult long runs due to dehydration and shriveled, drying, old, leather-like skin ... or so they say.
- You must eat fruits and veggies or will suffer a lack of energy and not get up the hills or finish the long runs.
- You must cut back on caffeine. In my game, I think both of my beasts are addicted to coffee. When I want another cup of joe, I am never too sure if it's physical or mental."

"In trying to satisfy these rules over the last week, I've found that low-fat cheese is much like eating a substance meant for sneaker production. I've also found that my brain is persistent and annoying when walking past a Mister Softee ice cream truck. I hear comments from inside my head sounding like 'Go ahead, the cones are small, there's protein in ice cream, isn't there? Don't be so joyless, girl, it's only a little ice cream for God's sake.' Unlike my mind, my body remains mute at the moment when I am cheating it out of the fuel it needs. It is silent and doesn't complain at all. Until later, that is, when it refuses to keep running or stay awake when I need it. So I have to remember that the effects of my bad food decisions are not immediate, but I'll eventually feel them."

"Obviously, the solution is to eat foods that taste good and are healthy. Maybe it's not that difficult and I am making a bigger deal out of this than I should. I can't really say since I've never tried very hard to find these foods before. I have a few in my collection and am building my repertoire daily. I still hate lima beans and peas, and I don't intend to even try changing those long-standing prejudices. But I have recently discovered tofu and am serving two vegetables at my dinner table instead of one, thanks to Liz Applegate's good advice. Who knows, maybe I'll even get adventurous at some point and try a spinach shake."

As can be seen; the discipline required to become a long distance runner is grueling, to say the least. After examining the discipline required to become a successful long distance runner, it is no wonder we are told in the scriptures: "Run with patience and endurance, the race that is set before you". Remember, the trophies one gains after this lifestyle of physical discipline, will mean nothing one day. The disciplines we endure for righteousness sake will last for all eternity. Compare the temporal with the eternal. There is truly no comparison.

Chapter #4

Discipline Of Athletes – A BODY BUILDER'S DISCIPLINE

Today, the physical fitness crave has literally hypnotized the world. People are willing to go through very arduous, intensely sacrificial and in most instances, painful and punishing processes to become physically fit – mind you, for personal gratification and self exaltation, to make oneself look good in the eyes of men. Let us examine the discipline required by a body builder to build muscles. Muscles become larger by being torn or ripped. What happens is: one has to build up the strength to lift heavy weights, for the heavy weights are required to tear or rip the muscles. After the muscles are torn or ripped, followed by the process of rest and healing, the muscles grow back larger. One cannot imagine the painful and punishing process of tearing muscles, resting and eating properly to acquire these sculptured bodies. Their mantra is the quote by the famous actress and singer Cher, in the Jack Lalane commercial of old – "No Pain No Gain". Only a body builder can attest to this truth.

Not only that, but in order to maintain these sculptured bodies this discipline must be maintained for a lifetime; for the moment one neglects to follow through with these disciplines, the muscles turns to fat.

The apostle Paul says these disciplines are done for a corruptible crown. We discipline ourselves: first of all, to make our Commander-in-Chief, the Lord Jesus Christ look good, thereby bringing Glory and Praises to Him; secondly, to receive an incorruptible, everlasting, and eternal crown. Glory be to God! It is interesting that, as in the case of most so-called "modern discoveries", the Bible has something to say on this matter. In scriptures we are told, "Physical exercise profiteth little, but Godliness is profitable for all things" (1st Timothy 4:8). The story of runner Jim Fixx best illustrates this point. The physical fitness craze began in the mid 1980's, with author and runner Jim Fixx, being its pioneer. The mantra was: "Becoming physically fit makes your heart stronger", thus making the athlete less likely to experience heart complications. Well, arguably, the most physically fit runner of his day, Jim Fixx, while running, died of a heart attack. The Word of God, as it has done from its inception, proves true – physical exercise truly profited little.

Chapter #5

Discipline Of Believers
PRAYER AND FASTING

Prayer can be defined as: the natural and honest pouring out one's heart to God. Prayer is the most necessary, but neglected, aspect of a believer's life, when, in fact, it should be the most important. Many believers do not realize the powerful and infinite resource available to us, through prayer, especially corporate prayer (Prayer where all believers are praying for a common cause). We acknowledge the fact that the country with the most nuclear weapons is the most powerful force on earth. That might seem true, from an earthly perspective, but the reality is, the most powerful force on earth is a praying believer. Prayer is the most powerful force available to man, more powerful than any nuclear weapon. Why? Because prayer is the force which moves the hand of God, and God is the most powerful (the only all powerful). We need to spend as much time in prayer as we do in the Word of God, if not more. The scriptures tell us, "The effectual fervent prayer of a righteous man availeth much"

Christian Soldiers

(James 5:16). We also see this truth in the book of Acts. Paul and Silas were in prison, where they began singing, praying, praising and worshipping God (Acts 16:25,26). The other believers were also praying for them, when, the scripture tells us, the entire prison shook and the doors were open. God speaks to us when we read His Word – the Bible. We speak to God when we go to him in payer.

Two words which best summarize a sermon on sanctification are: "Trust and Obey." We are told in Scripture, "as obedient children not conforming to the former lust…" If we simply trust and obey God, we would have no problem being the kind of person Christ wishes us to become. It is as we obey His Word, in childlike faith, we see that He is faithful, and our faith grows. As our faith grows, we trust and obey Him more, and the cycle continues. In the process, we grow to be more Christ-like. Glory be to God! The reality is: you cannot trust and obey someone you do not know, and you cannot know someone you are not communicating or spending time with. Just as we need to see Him for who He is – holy, in order to see ourselves as we are – sinful, we need to get to know Him for what he is – trustworthy and faithful, in order to trust and obey him the way we should – immediately and unconditionally. For the believer, prayer is actually the battle. When a believer is praying, he is battling spiritually. In the list of amour we are told to put on, in the book of Ephesians, we see that believers are actually in the battle when in prayer. The Greek word used for prayer in the book of Ephesians, actually denotes a struggle (Ephesians 6:18). A believer in prayer can be compared to a wrestler in a physical wrestling match. Remember, the battle is spiritual, the scripture says: "We wrestle not against flesh and blood". Prayer is: the natural outpouring of oneself to the creator God through Jesus Christ, for it is only because of what Christ has done on the cross, for our sins, that we can even approach a Holy God.

It is very easy to get distracted when praying. A method that was recommended to me and has transformed my prayer life is worthy of mention. This system has worked for me; it is not guaranteed to work for you – let the Holy Spirit of God lead you. Use prayer as a time of prayer, praise and worship. When you are tempted to get distracted and end your prayer, begin to sing worship songs of praises to the Lord, then begin to thank him for things he has done for you, one by one. When you are focused again, go back to your prayer. Keep repeating this process over and over again, as the need arises, and the spirit leads you. A good scripture verse to begin your prayers with is Psalm 139:23, "Search me oh God and know my heart, try me and know my thoughts and see if there be any wicked way in me." A good meditation song to sing is, "Search me oh God and know my heart today, try me oh Father and know my thoughts I pray". Then, as the Holy Spirit reveals your sins to you, confess them to God, repent, and ask for forgiveness.

Christian Soldiers

One look at King David's life leads one to wonder why God, in scriptures, denoted him: "A man after my own heart", despite all of the atrocities he perpetrated. One look at the psalms gives us a clue. In the Psalms, we see that king David was a man of repentance. Reading the Psalms gives one a picture that king David, though he failed the Lord miserably, as we all do, was a man of genuine sorrow, brokenness and contrition, over his sins. Recall when the prophet was sent by the Lord to crown a King from Jesse's household. Jesse began by presenting the strongest, brightest and best of his sons, to no avail. When there was but one son left (David), he was reluctant to present him. It was not until the man of God informed him that God had not chosen any of his sons, already presented, that he acknowledged there was one more – "a mere Shepherd boy." Lo and behold! When the prophet laid eyes on David, he instantly acknowledged, "This is the one God has chosen as king." Herein lies the key! What the man of God said after: "For man looks at the outward, but God looks at the heart." Don't get me wrong. God does not wink at sin. King David committed some terrible sins, which he paid for dearly. He lost the son born out of the adulteress relationship. His children rebelled, and there was turmoil in his family, and his kingdom, until he died. If we do not deal with our sins God will deal with them for us. God forgives the sins, but we have to live with the consequences. Sin is never winked at, by a holy God; for the wrath of God was poured out on Christ at Calvary's cross for our sins. Sin must always be dealt with in God's economy. In the Scriptures we are told, "God does not require a sacrifice, but the sacrifices of God are a broken spirit and a contrite heart". We are also told, "Blessed are the poor in spirit for they shall see God." When we think of the sins we commit against our loving Father, we should be broken in heart and spirit, knowing that we have failed a holy God. The scriptures tell us that the Goodness of God should lead us to repentance. The Apostle Paul says, "For the love of Christ constraineth us", it motivates, it compels me (II Corinthians 5:14). Love truly conquers all.

An illustration which underscores how we treat our Heavenly Father, in this area, is as follows: Let's say you are the father of four sons. The first son refuses to acknowledge that you created him, or that you even exist. The second son acknowledges the fact that you exist, and that you created him, but says you have left him on his own to fend for himself, and there is no way for him to get to know you. He also says even if there was a way to get to know you, he is not interested in knowing his father. The third son says yes you created him, and acknowledges the fact that you exist; but believes he can do as he pleases, live as he pleases (whatever makes him feel good…), for he is in control of his destiny. The fourth son, the one that, not only acknowledges your existence and his dependence on you, but also acknowledges that he knows you in a personal way, and is in fellowship with you (believers) – he only comes to you when he is in need or in trouble, never taking the time to thank you for all you've done for him, and/or rest in your love. He just begs, and begs, and begs. How would you feel? That can be compared to how the world, and many believers, treat our holy, loving, merciful creator.

We are told in the Bible, "pray without ceasing" (I Thessalonians 5:17). We need to be constantly aware of, and acknowledge the existence and presence of God, all day long – every waking moment, minute by minute, day by day, week by week and year by year. Our battle is spiritual. Our enemy, Satan and his fallen angels are spirits (Ephesians 6:12). Our loving creator, Father and Commander-in-Chief is also spirit. The Bible warns us, "The weapons of our warfare are not carnal" (II Corinthians 10:4). Our armor is spiritual. We are told to, "Put on the whole armor of God" (Ephesians 6:11), then given a list. We are also eternal spirits in a temporary physical body. The Bible admonishes us to be innocent as far as evil is concerned, but knowledgeable as far as good is concerned. Therefore, where the Bible is silent we are to take the position laid down in the scriptures: "The hidden things belong to the Lord" (2nd Corinthians 4:6, 2nd Corinthians 11:13,14). But, we are given some insight, in scriptures, as to what is taking place around us in the spirit realm, to make us more aware, and better able to "stand", as the scripture says. I emphasize – **in Scriptures.** The Scriptures should be our only source and guide in this, and every other area, for knowledge in spiritual and physical matters, pertaining to this deceitful and deceiving world. We are admonished in scriptures: "Test the spirits." We are told that we walk by faith not by sight – faith in the objective, unchanging Word of God. When what we see or feel contradicts the Word of God, we are to stand on the Word of God and discard what we see as false. Physical reality and truth are not necessarily one and the same. The apostle Paul tells us that even if an angel from heaven preaches to us another Gospel, we are to ignore it as false, for Satan transforms himself into an angel of light. In the Word of God we are told that signs are for unbelievers. We are to scrutinize, minute by minute, day by day, week by week, month by month and year by year, everything we see, hear, and even what we feel; and test it by the Word of God. If it contradicts the Word of God, then it is not of the one true and living God, no matter how real it appears.

Scripture tells us, "the battle is the Lord's", but, this does not eliminate our responsibility as soldiers in the army of Lord; for we are also commanded by our Commander-in-Chief, "Be sober, be vigilant." If the master was to open our spiritual eyes to the conflicts taking place around us, in the spirit realm, we would see demons – Satan and his fallen cohorts – trying to trip us up, and make us fail the master's name. But, more importantly, we would also see – as in the Old Testament when Elijah asked the Lord to open the eyes of a man that was fearful – that they that are with us are, indeed, more than those that are against us. Also, truly, greater is He that is in us, than he that is in the world. The battle is for the souls of unbelievers and sanctification of believers. The devil cannot inhabit believers' bodies – for it becomes the temple of God at the new birth; and light and darkness cannot cohabitate – so he tries to control our minds, for that can be influenced from without. A simple flip through the television channels on any given night will attest to this fact. The devil knows that our thinking controls our actions; this is why he, through the world, bombards us with enticements of the flesh. We do not anticipate the consequences of our thoughts, as we do the consequences of our actions, because we can see the results of our actions, but our thoughts are intangible. The reality is, our actions are a consequence of our thoughts. We notice in the book of Matthew, when Jesus cast out the demon from the demon-possessed man, the scriptures says he was "found in his right mind."

Fasting is also a very important weapon in the believer's arsenal of spiritual disciplines. We are told in Matthew 4:1-2: "Then Jesus was led up of the spirit into the wilderness to be tempted of the devil, and when he had fasted forty day and forty nights, he was afterward hungry." Notice that Jesus fasted before He was tempted. In Matthew 17:21, when the disciples could not cure the demon-possessed lunatic, Jesus said to them, "howbeit this kind goeth not out but by prayer and fasting." Fasting is important and should be an integral part of the believer's life – fasting, led by the Holy Spirit, that is. There are times when the Holy Spirit will lead the believer to spend a period of self denial (for that is what fasting is), especially at times when we are seeking a breakthrough in prayer, or we find ourselves slipping, and allowing a besetting sin to dominate and characterize our daily life. Fasting is denying the flesh. The flesh seeks to dominate and have its own way. When we fast, we are subjecting the flesh to the spirit. When we deny the flesh, we must feed the spirit by prayer and scripture meditation. A point to note: When we fast, we are not fasting to gain merit points in the sight of God. We are doing it for ourselves – to make ourselves better able to "stand" in this spiritual battle, and become better servants, and more effective witnesses for our Commander-in-Chief. From scriptures, and our experience, we see that fasting seems to be especially needed and prompted in times of "spiritual warfare" and/or "spiritual strongholds." Remember, when the disciples could not cast out the demon and the Lord had to cast it out, He told them, "this type only goes out by fasting and praying" (Matthew 17:21). We see this spiritual battle, also in the Old Testament, when the angel of God was hindered, by the evil one, from reaching Daniel, to answer his prayer. The Bible does not state why prayer and fasting are effective in especially breaking down spiritual strongholds (direct attack of Satan and his cohorts), but the reality is, we do not realize the devastating effect fasting and prayer has on the forces of darkness, until we exercise this discipline. We are to obey in simple faith, as is the case with all of God's commands.

Chapter #6

Discipline Of Believers
BIBLE STUDY, MEDITATION AND SCRIPTURE MEMORIZATION.

The psalmist declares, "Thy Word have I hid in my heart that I might not sin against Thee" (Psalm 119:11). Scripture reading, meditation and memorization has to be a daily part of the believer's life, if there is to be spiritual growth. Again, the psalmist tells us, "Thy Word is a lamp unto my feet and a light unto my path." A newborn believer will have a natural thirst for God's Word – just as a newborn baby has a natural thirst for his mother's milk. In scriptures we are told, "desire the sincere milk of the Word that you may grow thereby." Due to the fact that we are daily feeding on the junk food of the world, that natural thirst for the nourishing, sustaining, life-giving food of the Word of God has been waned in the believer's life. There should have been a time in a believer's life when he or she could identify with the scripture which says: "But call to remembrance the former days, in which after ye were illuminated, ye endured a great fight of afflictions; partly, whilst ye were made a gazing stock both by reproaches and afflictions, and partly, whilst ye became companions of them that were so used" (Hebrews 10:32,33). I call this the salvation experience scripture. A believer should remember that time, when you first trusted Christ as savior, the zeal and fire you had for the things of God, and the Word of God. But, where are you now? Where are we all now? This author can remember a period, immediately after receiving salvation, when individuals literally ran when they saw me coming, for they knew they would hear the gospel. As a sad commentary on this author, there are times, now, when individuals are likely to react similarly, the difference being, in some cases, for the wrong reasons. I have to say with the Apostle Paul when he asked: "Who can rescue me from this body of flesh?" Then he goes on to say, "But thanks be to God." Our Commander-in-Chief is more than able! We limit Him in our finite minds; but really and truly, HOW BIG IS OUR GOD? He is bigger than finite minds conceive – much bigger than mortal tongues can tell.

That natural thirst for the Word of God can be restored. The believer simply needs to get back into the Word of God – back to the basics, plain and simple. By studying and meditating on the Word of God more, and more, and more, before you know it, what Jesus said in the book of Matthew becomes a reality: "Blessed are those who hunger and thirst for righteousness, for they shall be filled" (Matthew 5:6). And I will add with much reverence – through the Word of God, be filled. Growth does not take place in a vacuum. It takes place in the battlefield of life, especially for believers. A very interesting illustration I heard, on our local Christian radio station, illustrates this point well. The topic was "Dealing with being physically overweight". The pastor said that one of the reasons we overeat is because we do not drink enough water. He said one needs to drink water periodically during the day, especially before meals. He goes on to say the reason we overeat is because we are really trying to fill that thirst for water with food, hence we overeat. He said there are people who do not like to drink water – myself being one – but, we have a natural thirst for water, and we lose that natural thirst by drinking everything else. He advises that if we were to begin drinking water on a regular basis, eventually that natural desire for water will return, and we will eventually like it again. Well, this author had to try it, and to my surprise, guess what? It worked. This is the same with the Word of God. The Word is food for our spirit – eat it more, and you will see that natural desire return. This famous quote sums it up: "The Bible will keep you from sin or sin will keep you from the Bible". In scriptures we are told, "Sanctify them through Thy Word for Thy Word is truth" (John 17:7). We can glean, from scriptures, some revolutionary benefits of studying God's Word:

- Joshua 1:8 – The Word of God makes your way prosperous and gives success.
- Psalm 1:3 – The Word produces faithfulness.
- Psalm 119:11 – The Word keeps you from sin.
- John 14:21 – God reveals himself to keepers of His Word. To name a few…

In scriptures we are told that the Word of God is profitable for literally everything, "that the man of God may be thoroughly furnished unto all good works" (2nd Timothy 3:17,18). Glory be to God! What more do we need? We need to study it, and meditate and memorize its precepts, in order to help us to better understand and obey. Scripture memorization must also become an integral part of the believer's life. This is a very difficult area for many believers, including myself. A good discipline that was recommended to me, and has worked quite nicely, is as follows: Use the period, between attempting to go to sleep, and actually falling asleep, as a time to repeat the verses you are trying to memorize. Repeat those verses over and over again, until you fall asleep. Also, at times when you are waiting in lines, for whatever reason, instead of letting your minds wander and worry, again, simply meditate on the scriptures you are trying to memorize. The believer needs to meditate on scripture. Notice, I said meditate on "scriptures." Nowhere in Bible is the believer ever told to blank his or her mind. This is very dangerous, for you are opening up yourself up to evil influences and effects on the mind, in the believer's case. If you are not a believer, you are opening up yourself to the possibility of being indwelled by demons (fallen angels). The believer's body is the temple of God; therefore the believer cannot be affected, by demons, from within, but they can affect us from without. Scripture declares it, and our experiences confirm it. The more we keep our mind filled and saturated with the Word of God, the less room we leave for evil influences. Light dispels darkness.

In the following scripture: "The Word of God is quick and powerful" (Hebrews 4:12), the Greek "dunamis" gives us the English word "powerful." This is the same word we derive the word dynamite from. Dynamo, or Powerful, describes the Word of God. The Word of God is truly powerful. Let it begin to transform your life. We feed our spirits when we are in the Word of God, and when we pray to God, the Father, through his Son, to intervene on our behalf, and give us strength to withstand temptations. The Bible is a spiritual book, as was aforementioned. One needs to be a born again to comprehend, apprehend and appreciate its transforming power. The scriptures say, "the natural man cannot comprehend the things of God for they are foolishness to him, for they are spiritually discerned." The reality is: if you do not have the spirit of God living in you, the Bible is a dead book to you, and it will not make sense.

Chapter #7

Discipline Of Believers
SPIRIT FILLED

In this dispensation, there are many essential doctrinal truths the believer must comprehend and stand firm on, such as, the sufficiency and accuracy of scriptures, the eternal security of the believer, the power of prayer in faith, the voice of God and the work of the Holy Spirit. The evil one and his cohorts have tried to counterfeit and confuse these areas with false doctrines and experiences, leading some to neglect these teachings and others to go to the opposite extreme of corrupting these teachings with false signs and experiences. 1st Timothy 4:1 tells us, "Now, the Spirit speaketh expressly, that in the latter times some shall depart from the faith, giving heed to seducing spirits, and doctrine of devils; speaking lies in hypocrisy; having their conscience seared with a hot iron."

The filling and work of the Holy Spirit is one of the essential truths the believer must apprehend and appropriate, as directed in scriptures, to become the kind of servant our Commander-in-Chief wishes us to become – sanctified and authentic. Jesus told the disciples in John 14:15-18, "If ye love me, keep my commandments. And I will pray the Father, and He shall give you another comforter that He may abide with you forever; even the Spirit of truth; whom the world cannot receive, because it seeth Him not, neither knoweth Him; but ye know Him; for he shall be with you and shall be in you. I will not leave you comfortless: I will come to you." He then tells them in John 16: 7: "Nevertheless I tell you the truth; it is expedient for you that I go away; for if I go not away, the comforter will not come unto you; but if I depart, I will send Him unto you. And when He is come, He will reprove the world of sin, and of righteousness, and of judgment." Then they are told to wait for the Holy Spirit in Jerusalem, before our Lord's ascension in Luke 24: 49: "And, behold, I send the promise of my Father upon you; but tarry ye in the city of Jerusalem, until ye be endued with power from on high."

In the book of Acts, we see the initial outpouring of the Holy Spirit: "And suddenly there came a sound from heaven as of a rushing mighty wind, and it filled all the house where they were sitting. And there appeared unto them cloven tongues like as of fire, and it sat upon each of them. And they were all filled with the Holy Ghost and began to speak with other tongues, as the spirit gave them utterance." The miracles and signs that followed this initial act of the Holy Spirit's coming into the world were simply to confirm the initial outpouring of the Holy Spirit on earth. Evil spirits have tried to counterfeit, confuse and copy this initial act. This was a one-time act to confirm and verify its authenticity. That is precisely what we are told in Mark 16:19-20: "So then after the Lord had spoken unto them, He was received up into heaven, and sat on the right hand of God. And they went forth, and preached everywhere, the Lord working with them, and confirming the work with signs following them." We then see that every believer receives the Holy Spirit at conversion. In Ephesians 1:13 we are told, "In whom ye also trusted, after that ye heard the word of truth, the gospel of your salvation; in whom also after that ye believe, ye were sealed with that Holy Spirit of promise." Subsequently we are told to be filled with the Spirit, Ephesians 5:18: "And be not drunk with wine, wherein is excess, but be filled with the Spirit." We are then given the consequences of being filled with the spirit: "Speaking to yourselves in psalms and hymns and spiritual songs, singing and making melody in your heart to the Lord; giving thanks always for all things unto God and the Father in the name of our Lord Jesus Christ."

There are those who teach that there are signs and a feeling that accompany the filling of the Holy Spirit. A comparison of Ephesians 5:18-21 to Colossians 3:16-18 reveals an interesting fact. Ephesians 5:18-21 states, "And be not drunk with wine, wherein is excess; but be filled with the Spirit; Speaking to yourselves in psalms and hymns and spiritual songs, singing and making melody in your heart to the Lord. Giving thanks always for all things unto God and the Father in the name of our Lord Jesus Christ." And Colossians 3: 16-18 states, "Let the word of Christ dwell in you richly in all wisdom; teaching and admonishing one another in Psalms and hymns and spiritual songs, singing with grace in your hearts to the Lord. And whatsoever you do in word or deed, do all in the name of the Lord Jesus, giving thanks to God and the Father by Him." An even closer inspection reveals a very striking parallel. Notice the progression:

Ephesians 5:18 to 6:20 – BE FILLED WITH THE SPIRIT

- Speaking to yourselves in Psalms and Spiritual songs.
- Singing and making melody in your hearts.
- Giving thanks always for all things.
- Husband and wives Submit and love one another.
- Children obey your parents and honor thy father and mother.
- Fathers provoke not your children to wrath.
- Servants obey your masters as onto the Lord.
- Be strong in the Lord and the power of His might and put on the whole armor.
- Pray for Paul that he may speak the Word boldly.

Colossians 3:16 to 4:4 – LET THE WORD OF CHRIST DWELL IN YOU RICHLY

- Teaching and admonishing one another in Psalms and Hymns and spiritual songs.
- Singing with grace in your hearts to the Lord.
- Do all things in the name of Lord.
- Giving thanks to God and the Father by Him.
- Husband and wives submit and love each other.
- Children obey your parents.
- Fathers provoke your children not unto wrath.
- Servants obey your masters as unto the Lord.
- Do all as unto the Lord.
- Masters treat servants properly.
- Continue in prayer and watch in the same with thanksgiving.
- Pray for Paul that the door may be opened for him to preach the Gospel.

Notice the parallel in the two above mentioned passages. First we are admonished to be filled with the Spirit, and then we are given the consequences of being filled with the Spirit. Then we are told to let the word of Christ dwell in us richly (be filled with word), then we are given the consequences. Notice that the consequences are almost identical. **Being filled with the Sprit and being filled with the Word of God produce the same results.** We can conclude that being filled with the Spirit is a result of being filled with the Word of God. Glory Hallelujah!

These are the results of being filled with the Spirit:

- A joyful and thankful heart.
- A submissive spirit.

- Peace and contentment.
- Love in your heart.
- Christ-like living.
- Power to witness about Jesus.

A comparison of Acts 1:8 and Luke 24: 47-49 reveals another hallmark of being filled with the Spirit.

Acts 1:8 states, "But ye shall receive power, after that the Holy Ghost is come upon you; and ye shall be witnesses unto me both in Jerusalem, and in all Judea, and in Samaria and unto the uttermost part of the earth." Luke 24:47-49 states, "And that repentance and remission of sins should be preached in His name among all nations, beginning at Jerusalem. And ye are witnesses of these things, and behold, I send the promise of my Father upon you; but tarry ye in the city of Jerusalem, until ye be endued with power from on high."

- The Holy Spirit produces power to witness about Jesus and the Gospel.

John 14:26 states, "But the comforter, which is the Holy Ghost, whom the Father will send in my name, He shall teach you all things, and bring all things to your remembrance, whatsoever I have said unto you.

John 15:26 states, "But when the comforter is come, whom I will send unto you from the Father, even the Spirit of truth, which proceeded from the Father, He shall testify of me and He shall also bear witness, because ye have been with me from the beginning."

Revelations 19:10 states, "…For the testimony of Jesus is the spirit of prophecy."

- The Holy Spirit reveals the truth of Jesus Christ and the Gospel, as revealed **in the Word** of God; not apart from or in addition to the Word of God.

John 16:8 states, "And when He is come, He will reprove the world of sin, and of righteousness, and of judgment."

- The Holy Spirit reproves the world of sin, righteousness and judgment.
- The Holy Spirit reminds the believer of sin and righteousness.

Romans 8:16 states, "The Spirit itself beareth witness with our spirit that we are the children of God."

- The Holy Spirit assures us of our salvation or our sonship.

1st Corinthians 2:9 states, "But as it is written; eye has not seen, nor ear heard, neither have entered into the heart of man, the things which God hath prepared for them that love Him. But God hath revealed them unto us by his Spirit, for the Spirit searcheth all things, yea the deep things of God. For what man knoweth the things of a man, save the spirit of man which is in Him? Even so the things of God knoweth no man, but the Spirit of God. Now we have received, not the spirit of the world, but the spirit which is of God; that we might know the things that are freely given to us of God."

- The Holy Spirit reveals to the believer the Glories of heaven that awaits us. Glory Hallelujah!

Galatians 5:22-23 states, "But the fruit of the Spirit is love, joy, peace, longsuffering, gentleness, goodness, faith, meekness, temperance; against such there is no law."

- The Holy Spirit produces the nine Christ-like temperament traits in the believer.

The Bible clearly teaches that a person is automatically, instantly, filled with the Holy Spirit, the moment that person places faith in Jesus Christ, as savior. The scripture says, "you are sealed with the Holy Spirit of promise" (Ephesians 1:13). Scripture tells us, "if you don't have the Spirit you are none of His" – you are not saved. Subsequently, it is a matter of continuing to be filled. We receive every bit of the Holy Spirit we will ever receive at salvation. Positionally, that never changes, but practically, His control – or complete dominance – is determined by our thoughts, actions and will. What we are commanded is: Continue to be filled – continue to be under the dominance or influence of the Holy Spirit (Ephesians 5:18). It is no surprise that being filled with the spirit is compared and contrasted with being under the influence of alcohol. Most of us, prior to salvation, can attest to the effects of being under the influence of alcohol. When drunk, you are totally under alcohol's control, to the point where you do not control your very actions. This is what we are called to do as believers. Do not confuse the issue; we do not become robots, for God never supersedes our will/intellect. He does not superimpose/force His will on us. Those are the actions of evil spirits (Demons).

It is that as you are filled and controlled by the Spirit of God, the Spirit's control becomes dominant to the point where you exercise your will to make decisions that are in conformity to God's Word, and will. You also become pre-occupied with seeing God's will for your life fulfilled. The Holy Spirit lives in us, but the believer needs to have every thought, word, and action, not only scrutinized by, but influenced, and dominated by Him. In many churches today, being filled with Holy Spirit is said to be complimented and confirmed by external signs. The devil tries to keep men from receiving Christ as savior. If he fails in this regard, he then tries to keep believers from understanding the importance and work of the Holy Spirit. One of the false impressions gained from man, not from the Word of God, is that a special feeling overwhelms the believer, when filled with the Holy Spirit. The words of God are objective truths directed to our intellect and minds, to be apprehended and obeyed, not to our feelings for subjective fulfillment and verification. There are four specific results of being filled with the spirit that are all guaranteed by the scriptures, and complimented by the believer's experience.

As was mentioned earlier, a believer is automatically filled with the Holy Spirit at salvation. Being filled continuously is an issue as to how much we allow the spirit to totally control, use and influence us. We do not need more of the spirit, for we receive all of the spirit when we are saved; it is a matter of the Spirit getting more of us. If the believer's life is characterized by the above mentioned consequences of the spirit, then you are filled with the spirit; if not, then you need to be obedient to the master and 'Be filled with the Spirit", an imperative in the Greek – a command. 2nd Timothy 2:21 tells us that the Holy Spirit only fills clean vessels. Positionally, our righteousness is Christ; for those that are in Him are safe and secure for all eternity. The scriptures say, "There is now therefore no condemnation to them that are in Christ Jesus." We are also told, "neither life, nor death …can separate us from the love of God that is in Christ Jesus." Practically, our righteousness is confessing our sins. 1st, John 1:9 says: "If we confess our sins, He is faithful and just to forgive us our sins and cleanse us from all unrighteousness." The believer's confessing of sins is not unto salvation, for that is settled at conversion. It is unto sanctification. Glory to the Lamb!

Please take a Look at some revolutionary benefits of studying the Word of God.

John 15:3 – The Word cleanses us.
John 15:7 – The Word produces power in prayer.
John 15:11 – The Word brings joy to our hearts.

1st John 2:13-14 – The Word gives victory over the wicked one.

The believer is to be careful not to Grieve the Holy spirit as is mentioned in Ephesians 4:30-31, nor quench the spirit as mentioned in 1st Thessalonians 5:16 and Philippians 4:6-7.

One author states, "Unless you let the power of God within you change your thinking pattern, your condition will gradually ruin your health, mind, business, family, ministry, and stagnate your spiritual growth." Truly, obey as obedient children and be transferred by the renewing of your mind. Glory Hallelujah to the spotless Lamb of God!

Chapter #8

The Discipline of Believers
Renewing the Mind, and Having the Mind of Christ

The Scriptures say, "I beseech you therefore brethren by the mercies of God that you present your bodies a living sacrifice, wholly and acceptable unto God; which is your reasonable service. And be not conformed to this world, but be ye transformed by the renewing of your mind, that ye may prove what is that good and acceptable and perfect will of God" (Romans 12:1).

The reason many believers are duped into believing they can live the Christian life, a life of pleasing God, on their own, is because the focus is on external behaviors and religious observances, instead of focusing on God's perfect law of love and purity of heart. The believer is transferred when a decision is made to subject his or her mind to the spirit of God, through the Word of God, to be transformed to the image of God. The closer one gets to a Holy God, the more acute the awareness of the sin within becomes. What can be perplexing, especially to a new believer, is the fact that when we first receive salvation, we really become fired up for the things of God, but then what happens? Notice in Hebrews 10:32: "The willingness to suffer for the Lord." But, when the honeymoon is over, and the reality of living in this fallen world sets in, and we begin to fail the master terribly – or should I say the reality of this becomes more apparent – even though we really, genuinely, desire to please Him, and are probably sinning less; this can lead the new believer to get discouraged and despondent. You need not be. The apostle Paul penned it like this: "What I would, do I not, and what I would not that I do." You see, the closer you get to a Holy God, the more you become acutely aware of the sin within. You do not see yourself as righteous, you see imperfection.

A better understanding of this principle can be gleaned from the following illustration: Take a white shirt that has been worn, but is relatively clean. Examine that shirt under normal light, and it will appear clean. If you examined that same shirt directly under a fluorescent light, I am sure you would see the imperfections. Better yet, examine it under a microscope, and you would be surprised as to how dirty that white "looking" shirt really is. The closer we get to a holy God, the more sin is revealed. Light reveals darkness. The more we see God for what He is – holy, the more we will see ourselves for what we are: Wicked and sinful. This is not meant to drive us away from the master in despair and dejection. It is meant to drive us closer to the master, in subjection and submission. Let's say you were on a boat. The boat sank, and you were able to keep yourself afloat on an inner tube, making that inner tube the sole instrument keeping you from drowning. You then get adventurous and try to swim away from the inner tube, only to realize, to your dismay, you cannot swim. What would you do? You would get back to that inner tube as quickly as possible, and hold on for dear life. I doubt whether wild sharks would be able to pry you away from that inner tube. As believers, we cannot live the Christian life in of ourselves. Just like the drowning person, we cannot swim. We need to hold on – or should I say, let the master hold on to us – for dear life. It's a good thing He is holding us, and not us holding Him. He has promised in His Word: "None can pluck us out of his hands." Glory Hallelujah!

God says He is the vine and we are the branches (John 15:1). We need to constantly, and vigilantly abide in that vine; for what the Lord says will never change while we are on this earth, in this fallen body: "Without me you can do nothing" (John 15:5), but Glory to God, He goes on to remind us: We can do all things through Christ Jesus which strengtheneth us (Philippians 4:13). The reality is, as the scripture says, we sin because we want to sin, and because we love it – not because we have to. We are told in Galatians 5:16, "Walk in the spirit and you shall not fulfill the lust of the flesh." In James 4:7,8:

"Submit yourself therefore to God. Resist the devil and he will flee from you. Draw nigh to God and He will draw nigh to you." We've heard popular phrases like: "The devil made me do it." No man can say the devil made him do anything; for in the Bible – I call this the LSD (Lust to Sin to Death) in scriptures – it states: "Let no man say when he is tempted, he is tempted of God" (James 1:13). Notice, the scripture continues: lust, when it is conceived leads to sin. So, we can see, the initial thought is not sin in itself. As one author said, "We cannot prevent birds from flying over our heads, but we can keep them from nesting there." The bad thoughts will appear. This, in large part, has a lot to do with what we feed our minds, and the old nature. Evil thoughts come from ourselves (within), and from the world and devil (without). An evil thought is not sin at its inception. It becomes sin at the point where we capture or appropriate (make a part of us) it. That is when sin has conceived. There is a point when the thought gives birth, or is conceived, and then it is sin. The scripture tells us, one cannot take fire to one's chest and not get burned, and we know from scripture and experience, when birth has been effected there has to be a death, otherwise it will grow to maturity.

Evil thoughts, I know, can be troubling, especially to a new believer, a babe in Christ. The fact that these terrible thoughts simply, suddenly appear, as from the pits of hell itself, can be perplexing. You need not feel guilty; for these thoughts are not necessarily your thoughts, that is, until you capture and dwell on them. The good news is that, you do not have capture and delight in them. You can capture and demolish them. God has provided the remedy, as he has in all areas of the believer's life. The solution is found in, and through, the Word of God. We are told in scriptures, "God will not allow you to be tempted more than that you are able, but will always provide a way of escape" (1st Corinthians 10:13). The old adage, "prevention is better than a cure", rings through; for it is easier to manage evil thoughts before they are formed, than trying to control them after they have given birth. Herein lies the simplicity of God's wisdom, which confounds the wisdom of this world. The Word of God destroys evil thoughts before they give birth. In the gulf war, Sadam Hussein launched scud missiles to destroy Israel. The Israelis' defense was a missile defense system called patriot batteries. After the scud missiles were launched, patriot missiles were counter-launched, immediately. The patriots intercepted the scuds in the air, and destroyed them, before they reached their intended target. We are told in II Corinthians 10:5: "Casting down imaginations and every high thing that exalts itself against the knowledge of God and bringing into captivity every thought to the obedience of Christ Jesus." Notice that these thoughts can be brought to the obedience to Christ. How do we cast down imaginations? How do we bring down these scud missiles of terrible thought, trying to give birth to sin; which would cause us to become spiritually ineffective in the Kingdom of God, by leading to terrible actions in our lives? We use the Word of God.

In Hebrews 4:12, we are told: "For the Word of God is quick and powerful, sharper than any two-edged sword, piercing even to the dividing asunder of soul and Spirit and joints and marrow, and is the discerner of the thoughts and intents of the heart." Notice that the dynamo – the powerful Word of God – pierces to bones and marrow. When unholy thoughts pass over our heads or come out of our flesh (fallen nature), we are to quote scriptures, especially those that apply to our hearts and minds. Hence, the believer needs to memorize scriptures, so that in the time of need, they are readily available (Psalms 119:11). Jesus gave us the example when the devil tempted him. Every time the devil misquoted scripture, (notice that he is true to his nature: a liar, a deceiver, just as he was to Eve in the garden) the Lord quoted the scripture accurately. The Lord said: "Away from me Satan, for it is written…." What glorious words; for, it is written indeed! Glory hallelujah! In scriptures we are also told, "Submit yourself to God, resist the devil and he will flee from you, draw nigh to God and He will draw nigh to you" (James 4:7, 8). In similar manner, the scud missiles are intercepted by the patriot batteries and destroyed in the air, before they can land and cause damage. The believer needs to scrutinize every thought, minute by minute, day by day, week by week, year by year, and take them captive, or demolish them, with the Word of God, rendering them harmless. Hallelujah! Oh the infinite wisdom of the riches of God! A large part of the problem is: Before we became believers, our minds have been conditioned to accept these devilish thoughts as our own; along with the lie that there is nothing we can do about them. We need to retrain our minds. Our minds need to be "transformed" by the Word of God, through arduous discipline.

In the field of psychiatry, psychiatrists have discovered that our actions are controlled by our thoughts, and that we can change our actions by changing our thoughts. Again the scripture has always said, "For as he thinketh in his heart, so is he" (Proverbs 23:7) – another truth stated in the Bible and now validated by the experiences of sinful men. Changing the way we think will change the way we act. It is interesting to note that psychiatrist, David D. Burns, M.D., in his book, "The feeling Good Handbook", dealing with cognitive therapy, said of his experiments with people that have disorders or compulsions: "Whenever patients were given medications that were designed to alter their moods, there were definitely, measurable improvements in the patients behavior." But the interesting fact is, when a placebo (a substitute, that is essentially nothing, for it has no medicinal value) was administered (unbeknownst to the patient), the improvement in the patients behavior were just as measurable, and in some instances, more than when they were given the actual drug. It is truly, as the old adage states, "all in the mind." A word of caution: The Bible, nowhere, teaches positive thinking, as is being taught by many teachers of our day. Yes, we are told to, "Be careful for nothing"; but we are never told to deny reality as a means of creating a better reality. We have to be careful. We are instructed to subject our minds, through our thoughts and will, to the Father, through the Word of

God. We are to obey the truths of God's Word. Obedience to these truths will direct our emotions accurately, giving us the ability to walk correctly, according to the truths of God's Word, not according to the lie of our sinful, impressive emotions and feelings – knowing that God is truth, and in Him there is no shadow of turning, or wavering. Glory Hallelujah!

The thoughts that linger over our heads are largely dependent on what we are feeding our conscious mind, with our senses – eyes, ears, nose etc. The scriptures tell us that we will reap what we plant. We can plant the right thoughts, and reap the right actions. This is not a passive act. The Bible tells us that our minds must be transformed, by being renewed daily. We need to revolutionize our way of thinking. Scripture says as we think in our hearts so are we. The old adage: "Garbage in, garbage out" reminds us of this truth. You can accurately say to someone: Show me your thoughts and I will tell what you are doing, or as the popular phrase goes, how you are living. In her book, "What's On Your Mind?" Carolyn Crothers asks the following question: "If you had a screen on top of your head, which literally displayed your every thought, for everyone to see; your wife, kids, family, co-workers and friends, etc. Would they be proud of what they see?" God sees all. Nothing is hidden from his eyes. Think about it. Philippians 4:8 tells us what we are to fill our minds with. It states: "Finally brethren whatsoever things are true, whatsoever things honest, whatsoever things are just, whatsoever things are pure, whatsoever things are lovely, whatsoever things are of good report...think on these things." Notice the first test is truth. Jesus said, sanctify them through Thy Word, Thy Word is truth. First of all, we are to fill our minds with the Word of God, and the Lord promises that if we hide his words in our hearts, He will bring them to remembrance when we need them. How do we hide the Word of God in our hearts? By memorization. Every thought that hovers over our heads is to be stopped instantly. Your actions are literally that of a door man, or a bouncer; inspecting everyone seeking entrance to an event. Every thought must be put to the test of Philippians 4:8. Ask: Is it true, it honest ..., and last but not least, will it bring honor and glory to God?

We are told in the Bible: "Work out your own salvation with fear and trembling, for it is God who worketh in you both to will and to do according to His good pleasure" (Philippians 2:13). Notice! We are to work out what God has worked in. Salvation is free, but sanctification is not passive; it requires effort and work. The new believer, as he struggles to let the spirit control what he thinks, has to control what goes in. In the beginning you will be battling a lot of the old thoughts, placed in your long term memory, from years of bad conditioning of the mind. It is paramount that you control what goes in, hereafter. There is a popular children song that warns: Be careful little eyes what you see, be careful little ears what you hear, and be careful little feet where you go. The television programs we watch, the things we listen to, the places we go; all must be subjected to the test of Philippians 4:8. A poem from the caring institute sums it up quite nicely. It says: "Keep your thoughts pure because thoughts become words, words become actions, actions become habits and habits becomes character and character becomes destiny." Just as we are to pray continuously, our minds are to be continuously occupied with pure thoughts; otherwise we will not become the effective soldiers, our Commander-in-Chief, desires us to become.

As was discussed earlier, everything begins from within, from the heart and mind. The change has to come from within. Jesus said what comes out is what is in the heart, and that is what defiles a man. We know the fruit of the spirit mentioned in Galatians 5:22, 23: "Love, Joy, Peace, Longsuffering, Gentleness, Goodness, Faith, Meekness, Temperance." We desire to exemplify these traits by trying to suppress those works of the flesh mentioned in Galatians 5:19-21: "Adultery, fornication, uncleanness, lasciviousness, idolatry, witchcraft, hatred, variance, emulations, wrath, strife, seditions, heresies, envying, murder, drunkenness, reveling." But those attempts are like sealing a pot of boiling water. You cannot see inside, but the water is boiling and hot. To cool the water you must turn off the fire, the very source. The world does not need more social programs, better living conditions, more trinkets; we need new hearts. The Bible says, "The heart is deceitful and desperately wicked, who can know it?" (Jeremiah 17:9). Outward conformity to rules can be mimicked. In other words we can obey rules and do things that look good outwardly, but, inwardly, the motives are sometimes wrong – selfish, devilish and even deadly at times – clearly sinning in God's eyes. The first question we tend to ask ourselves is: What's in it for me? We do right because we love the Lord Jesus Christ, not because we wish to make ourselves look good in the sight of men, or are fearful of being punished. God does not punish His children. He disciplines (trains) us to make us better.

In Matthew 6:33, we are told to: "But Seek ye first the Kingdom of God and His righteousness and all these things shall be added unto you." People took notice that the apostles were with Jesus after they saw that scared bunch of men, who scattered and denied the Lord, after his crucifixion and burial, later became bold witnesses for Him, after His resurrection. The apostle Paul started doing the opposite of the evil he perpetrated before he met the Lord. These individuals' lives were totally transformed – almost to the point of being opposite of what they once were. The Bible says, "If any man is in Christ he is a new creature, old things have passed away, behold all thing have become new" (2nd Corinthians 5:17). We cannot control our automatic feelings and reactions by will power. It must be done from within, by replacing bad thoughts with good ones. We do not change bad habits from without, but we prevent their formation from within. We believers must change what we allow into our minds. A total revolution has to take place. We need to change the old wicked way of thinking, which will eventually result in a change of our actions (Romans 12:2). The Greek word "metamorphosis" gives us the English word transformed, in scriptures. Metamorphosis is a very strong word. It literally denotes a radical change. Notice that the apostle Paul was said of, in scriptures: "The very doctrine and people he sought to destroy, he now preaches, and identifies with." Hallelujah to the lamb!

The popular T.V. program, the Incredible Hulk, illustrates the change metamorphosis denotes. Basically, the program centered on a news reporter, who, due to an accident with radiation, literally became transformed, from a calm, quiet, mild-mannered individual, to a ravenous, dangerous wild beast, whenever he became angry. This is an example of metamorphosis. This illustration is actually a reverse of what, ideally, should take place in the believer's life, after conversion, or the new birth. The desire to sin comes from within self (old nature). The temptation to sin comes from the world and devil. The desire to do right comes from the Lord, and the desire to do right is also in the believer, in the form of the Holy Spirit (new man). Our will makes the ultimate decision. We have a choice to make. We are not mere, mindless robots that have to be controlled by our emotions. We can do right – but by the grace of God. Hallelujah to the Lamb! A humbling experience, in this author's life, illustrates this point well. This author literally grew up on the mean streets of New York City and was literally lifted out of the pit of sin. Due to the depth of my transformation, I am prone to try to justify my, sometimes, disobedient actions, with statements like: "I've come a long way and some things are deeply rooted." Or: "I am not as bad as I used to be".

Christian Soldiers

I was having a conversation with my pastor, concerning sin, when I essentially told him that he couldn't imagine the dynamics of the things I am struggling with, from my past life. I was humbled when the pastor reminded me of a truth I know well. He stated: Though he admits that he does not know the dynamics of the things I am struggling with, from my past, he does know the Dynamo (power to change lives and keep one from sin) of the Gospel. Well, this author could not utter a word in reply; for I know the Dynamo of the gospel. Anyone that has trusted Christ as savior, thereby experiencing the new birth, knows the Dynamo of the gospel. There is truly no excuse. Just do as the scriptures say: "As obedient children not conforming to the former lust." Just believe and be saved, and just obey and be sanctified. Hallelujah to the Lamb!

Growth does not take place in a vacuum. In Proverbs 16:32, we are told: "He that is slow to anger is better than the mighty; and he that ruleth his spirit, than he that taketh a city." We are also told: "Let this mind be in you, which was also in Christ Jesus" (Philippians 2:5). Christ's ministry was hallmarked by serving others, exposing falsehood, giving hope to the weak, standing for the truth despite consequence, and sacrificing himself so others could live. Sins are only the symptoms. The disease is our wicked hearts, which contaminate every aspect of our being. Trying to stop sinning from the outside is like trying to stop up one's nose to cure a cold. The cold has to be dealt with from the inside. It can also be compared to one trying to earn his way to heaven, by his own righteousness. The Bible tells us that "all our righteousness is as filthy rags." This unknown quote sums it up: "The heart of the human condition is the condition of the human heart" (Isaiah).

At salvation, the Holy Spirit operates on our soul. Romans 2:28 states: "circumcision of the heart by the Spirit." This operation gives the believer freedom and liberty, from the flesh and ways of the world. Prior to the new birth, the problem was not our sins. Sins are simply the symptom. The problem was our wicked heart. When we trusted the Lord as savior, the Bible teaches that God gave us a new heart, called the divine nature. At salvation, the heart problem is solved. The victory over sin now comes through renewing of the mind in childlike obedience. We must change our way of thinking. There is a big difference between having a settled disposition to do wrong – regardless to consequences – and having a settled disposition to do right – but end up doing wrong at times. At the new birth, our attitude towards sin is no longer one of indifference. Sin no longer becomes a delight we take pleasure in; it becomes a burden we dread and regret. We are told, in scriptures, to present our bodies as living sacrifices, which is our reasonable service. We can all agree that it is more than reasonable, in light of what the master – our Commander-in-Chief, has done for us.

When one first begins the discipline of renewing the mind and guarding the senses, it seems, initially, like nothing is happening. Don't give up. Trust God; have faith in Him.

Christian Soldiers

Believe it or not, simply not giving in, or not reacting to a temptation, the way you once did is a victory in of itself. Though you may give into that temptation later, the fact is you have resisted it once, and you can resist it again, by the grace of God. Then, twice, then three times, and before you know it you've got total victory. Victory is built one step at a time. As you continue the discipline or training in the Word of God, through the spirit, you will have lasting victory. Notice that in the amour of God, listed in the scriptures, is our shield is faith. Why do we need faith as our shield? Because the devil throws darts of doubt to get us discouraged and give up our discipline for the master, especially when we fail. When we fail, we are simply to get up, dust off our knees, and continue to crawl – eventually we will walk. You will see the rewards of your discipline. One of the reasons we tend to give up when disciplining ourselves, especially spiritually, is because little tangible, definite benefit is seen initially. Don't give up; eventually you will see results. In the arduous discipline of a bodybuilder listed above, one does not see any immediate result as you go through the painful process of tearing muscles, but one day you look at yourself, and, voila, your muscles have grown. The same applies spiritually. You are being conformed to the image of Christ. Glory Hallelujah!

In Scriptures we are told: "The trying of your faith is more precious than gold." Trust God, you are being renewed inwardly. Disciplines are especially hard in the beginning, but remember, the experts tell us that if you practice anything for 30 days it becomes a habit. When beginning a discipline, you are to start gradually. If you begin with too much, you will become overwhelmed and give up. As you progress, you increase your discipline gradually, proportionally. Discipline must become a lifestyle, and a lifetime commitment – until the master comes or calls.

We are willing to discipline ourselves – in all kinds of painful ways – when we wish to lose weight to fit into that new dress, or that new suit, in order to make ourselves look good in the eyes of man. But, when it comes to disciplining ourselves for spiritual benefits that will make our Lord and Savior Jesus Christ – our Commander-in-Chief – look good, it becomes a burden. This author can relate a personal story that illustrates this point. In a desire to participate in a sporting event, I began a very rigorous routine of discipline – jogging, exercising, eating properly, resting and many other painful regiments. After a few days, I was convicted by the Holy Spirit. The conviction was: here I was, ready to subject my body to painful routines to make myself look good in the eyes of men, but when it came to disciplining myself with the things of God, to make the master, our Commander-in-Chief, look good, I sometimes get weary. In any event I went through with the discipline and participated in the event. To my dismay, my performance left a lot to be desired. Glory to God! Just trust the Lord! He says, though we are perishing outwardly, inwardly we are being renewed and conformed to the image of Christ. Singing glory Hallelujah, Jesus set me free!

We are told in Galatians 5:19: The acts of the sinful nature are sexual immorality and the like. We are also told, what we plant we will reap. Ephesians 2:3-4 tells us, if we sow seeds to the sinful nature we will reap destruction. Ephesians 4:22-24 tells us, we used to gratify the lust of our sinful nature and follow, notice: "its desires and thoughts." Remember, the old self is being corrupted by its deceitful desires, to be made new in the attitude of your mind. We see the principle of the progression, and building of momentum, in sanctification. The scripture says: "just as you gave in to sin leading to death, so give in to righteousness to holiness." This poem by an unknown author sums it up nicely:

"Little by Little"

"Growing in Christ takes work every day,
reading your Bible, learning to pray,
build Godly habits seek help divine.
Great things are done one step at a time.

Little by little, inch by inch,
by the yard it is hard,
by the inch what a cinch,
never stare up the stairs
just step up the steps,
little by little, inch by inch.

When mountains tower rugged and high,
rise to the challenge look to the sky.
Trust in the Lord and start out to climb,
reach for the goal one step at a time.
Great things are done one step at a time.

Little by little, inch by inch,
by the yard it is hard,
by the inch what a cinch,
never stare up the stairs
just step up the steps,
little by little, inch by inch.
Little by little, what a cinch."

Chapter #9

DISCIPLINE OF BELIEVERS – ETERNAL VIGILANCE

The scripture says: "Be sober be vigilant because your adversary the devil walketh about as a roaring lion seeking whom he may devour."

We all know the famous quote: "The price of liberty is eternal vigilance." As believers we have been liberated from the dominion of Satan and sin, and set at liberty to serve God. But, the price is truly, eternal vigilance. In scriptures we are told: "Be sober and vigilant." The word vigilant comes from the word vigil, which means literally, staying awake for some purpose. The dictionary defines vigilance as watchfulness, or alertness. The definition gives vision to the actions of a sentry, or an armed guard – constantly on patrol, weapon in hand, walking up and down, back and forth, constantly seeking to detect and apprehend any intruder. This must be the attitude, towards our thoughts, in our minds. Every thought should be stopped, checked and put to the test of Philippians 4:8. Individuals who preach discipleship (follower of Christ), and do not follow through with the discipline required to transform one's character into Christ-likeness, end up becoming detriments to the army of God, bringing disrepute to the master, shame to oneself, and brothers and sisters, and end up being called hypocrites by the world. This can be compared to one claiming to be a body builder, but neglecting to go through the actual discipline of lifting weights, which is required to develop muscles, or maybe, merely going through the motions of lifting weights, sometimes. It will eventually show; for there will be no physical change in your body. The world knows what a bodybuilder should look like. Just as they know what a true disciple of Christ should look like. We need to be honest and wise about our struggles and victories, to believers and unbelievers. We are told in scriptures to: "Work out your salvation with fear and trembling." In order to become Christ-like, the believer must be completely vigilant in every area of life, every day of his or her life.

The Psalmist said, "I will set no evil before my eyes." We are later told in the Psalms: Write the laws of God on our doorposts, on our foreheads, literally everyplace that will afford us the opportunity to see them and be reminded of them. We are also told in scriptures to shun the very appearance of evil. A Christian should never have to say: "It is not what it looks like." If the appearance is there, then the potential to do evil is also there. The believer's life should be as transparent as can be, while remaining, as the Lord commands: harmless as a serpent and wise as a dove. Transparency protects us from having secret areas in our lives. Hidden areas make it easier for us to cover up sins. The scripture warns us not use our liberty as a cloak for evil (1st Peter 2:16). The believer needs to put up barriers, and set parameters so that we don't fall over the edge and protection, into sin. On roads, barriers are placed to protect vehicles from going over the side of the roads. To avoid sin, we may need stay away from certain individuals, certain places; in some cases it may take driving a different route to avoid temptations. Again, the psalmist warns: The wise man foresees evil and hides himself.

The experts tell us that by the time a decision gets to our will for a final decision to be made, our flesh, emotions and every other faculty of our fallen being have already conspired to get a response that will be favorable to them. The problem is not that we do not exercise our will, it is just that, we allow so much garbage in that it makes it easier for us to use our will to make the wrong decisions, when it is pressured by our fallen nature. We have to wake up every morning and say to ourselves: Winston I cannot trust you! And submit our entire being to God through prayer, Bible meditation and eternal vigilance. As was intimated in the previous chapter, the experts tell us that the outcome of the war has already been decided before the actual, physical battle takes place. The better trained and better prepared army has already won. The actual battle is almost a formality. Similarly with the choices we believers make, we begin by going through the rigorous discipline of preparing our minds and spirit, so that when we are faced with temptations, in any form, we have already purposed in our hearts, and decided what our reaction will be. Daniel purposed in his heart, and it enabled him to make the right decisions. When he was faced with the choice of being obedient to God or being obedient to man, he was able, by the grace of God, to obey God's Word.

Certain wrong actions should not even be an option in the believer's mind. The Bible tells us the temptations we give into are but distractions. We, through the spirit, can overcome; for Greater is He that is in us (1st Corinthians 14:15). An old comedy movie illustrates this point well. In the movie; a physical, mechanical giant went about the town, terrorizing and intimidating its inhabitants. The appearance of this giant was such that one look at him literally instilled fear into their hearts. The funny part came when, due to malfunction, the giant collapsed. We then saw a two foot midget walk out of the giant machine and run away. The giant was actually a midget masquerading as a monster. We believers encounter midgets, in the form of temptations, every day, and we give in to them. The reality is, we don't have to. The Bible tells us, greater is he that is in you than he that is in the world, and that God will always provide an escape from temptations (I Corinthians 10:13). It is interesting to note that in the computer technology, tampering with the wrong files – called system files – can have catastrophic consequences to the computer. So, in order to protect the computer, those system files are hidden. Until a technician, in his need to, enables options to make them visible, they are not visible. Also, making the wrong choices at certain stages in the operating of the computer, can have detrimental consequences; so, what the designers have done is, those choices are not an option at those stages of the operating of the computer, making it impossible for someone to make the wrong choice, at the wrong time. We, as believers, need to be so vigilant that certain wrong choices are not only not considered, but they are not even an option. We are to make them literally not available, by eliminating the option.

We can train our minds to convince our wills to make the right choices. That should be our mindset. Our will makes the decisions. The believer's life is about choices and making decision – the right ones, the ones that conform to God's Word and will, and will bring honor and glory to the our Commander-in-Chief, the Lord Jesus Christ, period. King David said in the Psalms, "one thing he desires and that will he seek after" (Psalm 27:4). Think of desiring one thing so badly, that you set your mind towards accomplishing that one thing. Your every conscious moment is spent towards accomplishing that task. You exercise all of your faculties to accomplish that one thing. In many cases, we are willing to do that for the things of the world, in order to bring honor and glory to ourselves. Why can we not do the same, in order to bring glory to our Commander-in-Chief? The scriptures say "Blessed are those who hunger and thirst after righteousness, for they shall be filled" (Matthew 5:6).

The believer has to be disciplined and vigilant in every area of his or her life. Every thought, motive, word and deed has to be scrutinized and controlled by the Holy Spirit. The victory has to be continuous. How do you continue to be victorious? The secret is: Simply continue to do what you have done. In scriptures we are told: "Do not be weary in well doing, for in due season, you will reap your reward" (Galatians 6:9). In the army of the Lord, it is not so much how you begin, but how you finish, that counts. One day we will hear the master say: "Well done good and faithful servant", and we will see that it was, indeed, worth it. We will see that, as the scriptures say: The sufferings were truly not worthy to be compared to glory that is revealed in me (Romans 8:18). We are told in scriptures: "Eye hath not seen nor ear heard, neither have entered into the heart of man, the things which God hath prepared for them that love him. *But God hath revealed them unto us by His Spirit: for the Spirit searcheth all things, yea, the deep things of God"* (1st Corinthians 2:9-10). We've won the victory, we are winning the victory, and we will win the victory – but by the grace of God! Glory, to the spotless Lamb of God.

Today, Coca Cola is probably the most recognized brand name the world over, yet continues to spend a lot of money on advertising. Legend has it that the CEO was asked, one day: Why do you keep spending so much money on advertising? You are already the most recognized brand, the world over? It is stated, the CEO's response was: "We continue to advertise, because that is how we continue to remain the world's most popular and recognized brand." For the believer, vigilance must become a minute by minute, day by day, week by week, month by month and year by year attitude of our minds and body, until the Lord Jesus Christ returns, or calls us home. A famous quote intimates that one can, "be too earthly occupied and become heavenly no good, or become too heavenly occupied thereby becoming earthly no good." The reality is that we can never be too heavenly occupied, so as to become earthly no good; for if we are truly "heavenly occupied", as we should be, everything on earth will fall into its proper place. Everything else will be, literally, in its proper perspective, absolutely. Scripture guarantees it and our experiences confirm it. The scripture says, "the prudent man foresees the evil and hideth himself" (Proverbs 27:12). Joseph literally ran to get away from the temptations of Pharaoh's wife. We are told: "FLEE also youthful lust" (II Timothy 2:22), "But SHUN profane and vain babblings" (II Timothy 2:16). The apostle Paul said: "I DIE daily" (I Corinthians 15:31). In Colossians 3:5 we are commanded: "MORTIFY therefore your members". These are very harsh words. The believer needs to have a constant awareness of the impending danger and destruction of sin, self, and the world; for the wages of sin is death. Remember, none of us – no matter how spiritual we think we are – are immune to any type of sin. The reality is, the potential is there for us to commit any sin committed by the worst in society. A believer can never say I would never do that. Our attitude should be: "but by the grace of God, I pray never do that." The Bible says pray, lest you be overtaken with the same sin. Abide in the loving vine, for the Lord Jesus alone gives victory.

The discipline of the Buddy system can be very beneficial to the believer who wishes to be the type of soldier our Commander-in-Chief desires us to become: Authentic person. This gives earthly accountability on a granular level. The idea is to find a godly person, one who is known for confidentiality and one you are certain you can trust with your very life. Your pastor, deacon or a member of your church would be ideal. If it has to be someone outside the church, make sure it's a born again believer, who is in close fellowship with the Lord. You are to hold yourself absolutely (as unto the Lord), accountable to this individual, revealing your every struggle. For this discipline to be effective, you must be absolutely honest about every aspect of your spiritual, personal, and private life. Ask this individual to keep tabs on you, inquiring as to your progress, from time to time. Someone in your church would be ideal, for it will keep you from having a secret or double life. Some spousal accountability can't hurt either. We should hold ourselves totally accountable, as far as time, resources etc. is concerned. We are to let our spouse know where we are at, and what we will be doing at all times we are not in their presence. We should even check in by way of phone call when we are away from them too long. We should let them know where every penny we have goes, and last but not least, we are never to keep secrets, nor ask anyone to keep secrets for us. This quote, from an interview with Charles Swindol, sums up the point: "I simply recognize that being a man, temptations is always on the back burner waiting to singe me. We need open accountability, regularly. I need friends to look across the desk, lean over, and say, I love you too much to let you live in an isolated world of dreams and fantasies. You are not doing that are you? And I need to say no, but keep asking me. I don't want to start doing that, it's almost an epidemic."

The Bible has a lot to say about the believer's walk, or conduct, or manner, or way of life. We believers need to be transparent in everything we do. Our every action should be open for all to see. Light dispels darkness. We need to walk in the light always as the scriptures say. 1st John 1:7 tells us: "...But if we walk in the light, as He is in the light, we have fellowship one with another and the blood of Jesus Christ His Son cleanseth us from all sin." In Scriptures day and light are used figuratively to represent good and truth; whereas night and darkness are used to represent evil. We are told in Ephesians 5:8: "For ye were sometimes darkness, but now are ye light in the Lord: Walk as children of light." Ephesians 4:1 tells us: "I therefore the prisoner of the Lord beseech you that ye walk worthy of the vocation wherewith ye are called. We are also told in scriptures to walk to please God, walk in truth and to walk in love.

We cannot, absolutely, protect ourselves from life's pitfalls; that comes from dealing with people. Remember, we are all sinful, fallen people – we are all Adam and Eve's children. First, we learn to be selective. Find Godly brothers and sisters who love the Lord, and are genuinely striving – and struggling at times, as we all are – to please Him. There will be times when you will both fail each other, but that is all part of the growth process. When we are wronged, we forgive and continue to grow in fellowship with each other and Lord. One author said, "To live above with saints in love, O what glory, to live below with saints we know, well that's another story." As believers we need to be transparent in all that we do. It will go a long way in aiding to protect us from ourselves. We are to be transparent in our relationships, jobs, ministry, and families – in a word, all. The discipline of vigilance of the believer is on at every waking moment of our lives: Every step we take. Every encounter we have. In the house, on the streets, in the car, at work; our every thought, motive, and action needs to be scrutinized and analyzed moment by moment, hour by hour, day by day, week by week month by month, and year by year until the master comes or calls. Remember, The Honor and Glory of our master's name is at stake. We are ambassadors of Christ. We should hear the master say every waking moment: Winston Do you love me? If you love me keep my commands. And again: Winston, Do you really love me? If you really love me meditate on my commandments. And yet again: Winston do you really, really love me? If you really, really love me, delight in my commands.

The wages of sin is death. It was the death of God's son Jesus Christ. If we continue to sin, without confessing and forsaking, it will be death of our testimony, and the death of our effectiveness as a soldier in the Army of the Lord. Suppose you were standing on the streets when an out of control car approached you, at a tremendous speed; what would you do? I can imagine the haste with which you would get out of the way would even surprise yourself. In Ephesians 6:11-13, we are told that we are fighting against a heavily arranged and organized spiritual enemy, hence our need to be eternally vigilant. Failures of the past can be a hindrance. Believers need to do as the apostle Paul: Forgetting what is behind and striving towards what is ahead. Forget about yesterday's failures and discipline yourself towards tomorrow's victory (Philippians 3:13). The Lord is more than able to keep. Glory Hallelujah!

Chapter #10

Discipline Of Believers – FELLOWSHIP

The scripture tells us that our relationship with God is not vertical, it is horizontal. Our relationship with our fellow man is a reflection of our relationship with God. It is not "me and God", upward. It is me and God, in the form of everyone we encounter. We are told in scriptures that we are liars if we say we love God, whom we cannot see, and do not love our fellow man, whom we see every day (1st John 4:26). The disciples were told by the Lord: When I was naked, you clothed me, and when I was hungry you fed me. They asked: When did this happen. Jesus' reply was: When you did it to the least of these your brethren, you did it to me (Matthew 25:35-45). The reality is: If our relationship is not right with our fellow man, it is, more than likely, due to the fact that it is not right with the Lord. And likewise, if our relationship is right with God, it will more than likely be right with our fellow men. If we are vigilantly pursuing the disciplines required to make us effective soldiers, effective for the master's use, our relationship with others will be what it ought to be. This author will tell you the times my relationship with my brothers and sisters is not what it should be, and the times I am the most selfish, are when my relationship with the Commander-in-Chief is not what it ought to be. Conversely, the times my relationship with my fellow man is anywhere near what it should be, are the times when my relationship with the Commander-in-Chief is shaping up to be close to what it should be – or should I say – the times it has a semblance of what it should be.

Fellowship of Believers

Fellowshipping with believers is a very important discipline for any soldier of the army of the Lord who desires to be effective. In scriptures we are told, "Iron sharpeneth iron" (Proverbs 27:17), and we are admonished to "not forsake the assembling of ourselves together" (Hebrews 10:25). A popular saying today is: "I don't need to go to church to be a Christian." Though that may be correct, for the believer's body is the temple of God, and the individual believer is actually the church, I would say the believer needs to go to church to look like a Christian, sound like a Christian, act like a Christian and walk like a Christian. We know the old adage: If it looks like a duck, walks like a duck, sounds like a duck, acts like a duck and quacks like a duck, you need not ask what it is. God has ordained the Church as means of nourishment for the believer. We are fed the Word of God in church. We need to be reminded, and reminded, and reminded of the things of God. We are forgetful creatures. We forget more than we remember. Remember, we are transformed by the renewing of our minds. Again, we are forgetful creatures, and need to be constantly reminded, and reminded and reminded. The Church, or the assembling of believers, also provides protection for the believer. Imagine an animal, in the jungle all by itself. It becomes an easy prey to the stronger and predatory animals. The Church, or fellowship of believers, also provides accountability. We all need to be held accountable, especially this author. The worst thing the Lord can do to us is to leave us to ourselves, and let us have our own way. If we desire to be good soldiers of the master, there can be no such thing, as too much accountability.

The Church is not an organization. It is a living organism that is enriched, energized and enlightened by the Holy Spirit. The Word of God teaches that when one part of the body of believers hurts, all are affected (1st Corinthians 12:26). My actions, as well as your actions, both good and bad, affect the entire body of believers. We can literally say: The church is not what it should be, because of you and me. Another popular excuse for non-church attendance is: "I am not going to church because they are all hypocrites." One preacher said: If you find a perfect church don't join it because you will spoil it. Another preacher said he left one church for another, and tried to justify it to the Lord by telling Him that he left because they were all hypocrites. He was quite humble in relating that the Lord directed him to go back to that very same church, after informing him that he is a hypocrite also, so that is where he belongs. In the book of Genesis, after Cain slew his brother Abel, and the Lord inquired as to Abel's whereabouts, Cain flatly asked God if he is his brother's keeper. Well, the reality is that we are our brother's keeper. Our attitude should be that of the author who penned: To my God – a heart of flame, to my fellow men – a heart of love, and to my flesh – a heart of steel. One of greatest hindrances and damage to the effective and effectual fellowship of believers, I believe, is pride. Remember, this was the original sin. This is the sin that Lucifer introduced. There are no Big I's or small U's in the Army of the Lord. The ground is level at the foot of the cross. We are all co-laborers with the Commander-in-Chief. We are called to bear one another's burdens, to uphold those that are weak and to esteem others better than ourselves. We repeat things we hear about our brothers and sisters that may not even be true. We are to talk to God about man, and talk to man about God, period. Anything else is slander and gossip. In Galatians 6:1, we are told to restore our brother or sister in a spirit of meekness. We are to Pray for our brothers and sisters. The reality is, the brother or sister we are condemning, just might love the master more, and be closer to the Him, than you and I and may ever get. Think about it.

The Bible teaches that the tongue is an evil unto itself. The scripture says no man can tame the tongue (James 3:8), and then we are told, where words abound sin is found. When we speak too much, the danger is we may begin embellishing, then outright lying, possibly to make ourselves look good. We are to make sure everything we say or repeat passes the test of Philippians 4:8. Ask yourself: is it true, is it honest, will it uplift my brother or sister and most of all will it bring glory to the master? If we do not have anything good to say to or about our brother or sister – anyone for that matter – we are to simply be quiet, or to put it bluntly: Shut up. We have two ears and one mouth, why? The Lord is trying to tell us something. We are to listen more than we open our big mouths, this author especially. Sometimes I think I was born with foot-in-the-mouth disease. But thanks be to God! He is more than able to transform. Another interesting fact is that when we wake up in the mornings, our mouths normally do not smell too lovely; it literally needs cleaning, why? Because it stinks. Do you think the master is, again, trying to tell us something? In the scriptures we are told that, with our mouths, we bless God and curse man. One cannot imagine what an encouraging word can do to help, encourage and even uplift a struggling brother. The scripture says, a word fitly spoken is like apples of brass in pictures of silver. The opposite is also true. That is, how damaging a word out of place can be to a struggling brother, to the point of, possibly, causing him to stumble, or even worse, causing him to become discouraged and give up. Think about it – that brother for whom Christ died. My pastor always reminds me that we are to share the help not the hurts, the helper – the Lord Jesus Christ. Yes, in this life people will hurt us, and we will hurt

Christian Soldiers

people. The Bible says, "Be not overcome of evil, but overcome evil with good" (Romans 12:21). A good way to truly overcome anger towards an offending brother or sister is to think of a good deed that you can do for him or her, and do it. You will be surprised how that spirit of bitterness and resentment simply melts under the kind deed of a loving act. As the scriptures say, love truly overcomes. Also, pray for a person who has wronged you. If the person is not saved, pray for his or her salvation. If the person is saved, pray that the Lord would truly sanctify him, and make him – as he is doing in and with you – a better soldier, for His use. An unknown author penned these few words:

> "Take a little time today to mend a broken heart
> or gather up the pieces of a dream that's torn apart.
> Take a little time today to graciously
> extend an outstretched hand
> to someone who really needs a friend.
> Take a little time to make a life worthwhile
> for a stranger who can use an understanding smile.
> Reach for heaven and reflect the sunshine from above.
> Take a little time today to radiate God's love."

That sums it up nicely; for the mark of a Christian truly is love. The scriptures say, all men will know we are God's disciples, by our love one to another (John 13:35). The next time you see your brother sinning and you are tempted to say: "I don't believe that a Christian would do something like that." Just remember the times you've failed the master and could not believe you could have done something like that. Pray for your weak brother. Do not chastise or gossip. We are commanded to do nothing out of selfish ambition and vainglory, and to consider others better than ourselves.

Again, we are told in scriptures, iron sharpens iron. We believers are to watch who we fellowship with. The Bible asks, what fellowship does darkness have with light? We are to find godly brothers and sisters that are striving for righteousness to spend time with. They may not be perfect, but if you know they genuinely love the master, and genuinely have a desire to do right, and most of all – it shows, you are in good company. Believers are to put God first, others second and ourselves last. As fallen beings, we've got to be careful of what I call: "the Lucifer syndrome", the so-called "independent" or "self-reliant" spirit. The world exhibits this tendency in its quest to live independently of God, which is impossibility, for in Him we move and breathe and have our being (Acts 17:28). Believers exhibit this tendency in the form of so-called self-reliance. Lucifer thought to himself that he could be God, thereby not being dependent on God. We cannot live independently of God, whether or not we believe it. But God in His wisdom has ordained it that we cannot live independently of each other, either. We are all God's hands and feet on this earth. God has chosen to work through people – yes, fallen, sinful, people. He desires to do well for others through us, and do well for us through others. Remember, God softens hearts and hardens hearts. He hardened Pharaoh's heart. The Bible also tells us, God is for us among those that help us. This takes away the pride of self-reliance, and self-dependency. Phrases like: "I am a self-made man", "I did it my way" and "I am the creator of my own destiny", though they sound good, in reality are false. We are at the mercy of God, absolutely. We are not at man's mercy. Though he chooses to use man to carry out His will, it is nevertheless His will. This should reiterate the fact that we never have to compromise our principles or the Word of God to accomplish anything, or appease anyone. His counsel stands. He has designed it in such a way that we all need someone, and we all need each other. Who can boast? Oh the infinite wisdom of the master.

As was stated earlier, the church is a living organism not an organization. An organization is an organized whole, whereas a living organism is a dynamic living whole, where every member is unique, and equally important. In an organization, parts can be replaced and even substituted, and not dramatically or detrimentally affect the functioning whole. In some cases the organization may even function better. Not so in an organism. In the body of believers, each part is unique and irreplaceable. Each part is unique and has a unique role. If a part is not functioning correctly in an organism, the whole can never be what it is meant to be. We can thus accurately say that the church, today, is truly not what it should be because of its members, you and me. Each part is irreplaceably, and absolutely dependent on the other. Christ is the head, and we are never static in the body of Christ. We are either going closer to the world or closer to the master; moment by moment, day by day, week by week and year by year. In the great bye and bye when we are with the master, and as the scripture says, we will know as we are known, I believe we will see the dynamics of the consequences of our actions and inactions on the entire body of believers, and no doubt, will be resentful, remorseful and ashamed. We will see the missed opportunities to share and shine for the master. An organism is dynamic, always alive and growing, or dying. As believers we do not have rights. Even the most ungodly and perverted individuals are claiming "their rights", today. Our "rights", as believers is simply to "do what is right", as laid down in the Bible, God's Word, regardless of the cost or consequence to self, and leave the results to the Lord. Stand on God's Word and see how faithful He is!

Chapter #11

Discipline Of Believers – SEPARATION FROM THE WORLD

1st John 2:15-17, the believer is told: "Love not the world, neither the things that are in the world. If any man loves the world, the love of the Father is not in him. For all that is in the world, the love of the flesh, and the lust of the eyes, and the pride of life, is not of the Father, but is of the world. And the world passeth away, and the lust thereof: but he that doeth the will of God abideth for ever."

Our Commander-in-Chief, the Lord Jesus Christ has a lot to say about the world. The word "world" appears 258 times in the Bible, of which 206 are in the New Testament. Most of what the Lord has to say about the world is not particularly lovely. Yes, we are told in John 3:16: "For God so loved the world that he gave his only begotten son, that whosoever believeth in Him shall not perish but have everlasting life." But, the believer is commanded not the love the world. To understand our Lord's admonition, one needs to take a closer look at the scriptures. What, or who is the world? In the parable of the "Tares and the Wheat (Matthew 13:25)," we see that the field is the world. In Psalms King David admonishes: "let the wickedness of the wicked come to an end" (Psalms 7:9). As believers we are to love sinners, but not their sin. Most of all we are not to condone it in others and in our selves. Many believers are clearly violating the laws of God, because in their words: "We are not under the law", and "I don't practice legalism". We know that we are not under the law. The Bible is clear on that. But there seems to be confusion in this area. Legalism has to do more, with our motives, than it does with our actions. We obey God's commands because we love Him, not because we are trying to keep the law or gain merit points in the kingdom of God's economy. In these last days of enticements of the flesh, where is the difference and distinction of the believers and the victorious living the Bible promises to believers? Christians only look different on Sundays when we dress up with our best clothing and look holier than thou, then during the week we look and act like Lucifer himself. Heaven help us all who name the name of Jesus. Help us to depart from evil as the Bible commands. The solution is the eternal answer – But thanks be to God. It's not being a legalist when we willingly avoid people, places, and events, and dress modestly; because we believe it might cause us, our brothers and sisters, to bring disrepute to the name of God. It's called being wise, and as the apostle

Christian Soldiers

Paul says: We are our brother's keeper. The scriptures say, the wise man foresees evil and hideth himself. Wise – lock the door tight to avoid seeing evil – that kind of wise. There are times we have to look up or turn our gaze to the left or right to avoid seeing evil in these days of near nudity. Run, flee, shun, avoid; for such is the danger of sin. Similarly, we are not judging when we state facts. We are judging when we judge our brother or sister's motive, and when we take the attitude of a "Pharisee", over their shortcomings. We are to speak the truth when a brother or sister is clearly violating the Word of God – not in a spirit of superiority, but in a spirit of meekness and love, knowing that we can be overtaken in that very same temptation or maybe even worse.

Separation from the world is another one of the doctrines of the Bible that is neglected, because of excess of a few. Some teach that we are to be totally segregated from the world, which the Bible does not teach. We are told to be in the world but not of the world (John 17:16). Others teach that we have to mingle with the world in every aspect to get the gospel to them, even it means visiting many sinful, social places. This is not taught in the Bible either. In scriptures, we are told to come out from among them and be ye separate, and also we are also told not to be unequally yoked. In all excesses, there is always middle ground – a balance. In most cases, that is where we find the truth. The balance is: We need to be in the world, but selectively separate from the world. 1st Corinthians 5: 10-13 states: "I wrote unto you in an epistle not to company with fornicators: Yet not altogether with the fornicators of this world, or with the covetous, or extortioners, or with idolaters; for then must ye needs go out of the world. But now I have written unto you not to keep company, if any man that is called a brother be a fornicator, or covetous, or an idolater, or a railer, or a drunkard, or an extortioner; with such an one not to eat. For what have I to do to judge them also that are without? Do not ye judge them that are within? But them that are without God judgeth. Therefore put away from among yourselves that wicked person." This scripture is addressing Church discipline, which definitely needs to be taught and administered more in our churches today, but the crux of my argument, for this chapter, is the fact that, if the Lord wanted us absolutely, separate from the world, he would have taken us home to glory the moment we trusted Christ as savior. He has left us to be the salt of the earth, to proclaim the Gospel of His salvation with our lips, and especially our lives. The Lord said that the only way we cannot keep company with, or associate with unbelievers is if we were taken out of the world - hence the title of this chapter: "Separation from the world", or separate from, not segregation from, while in the world. This calls for believers to be, as the scripture says, harmless as a dove and wise as a serpent, and to walk circumspectly. We are not called to segregate ourselves, we are called to separate ourselves in areas that will cause us to compromise our scriptural convictions, and cause us to shame our savior's name. As a matter of fact, we are commanded, in scriptures, to shun the very appearance of evil. So, though we may be strong in certain areas, we are to subject our actions to the conscience of our weak brothers, as is stated in scriptures.

Ephesians 2: 2 states: "Wherein in time past ye walked according to the course of this world, according to the prince of the power of the air, the spirit that now worketh in the children of disobedience." In Ephesians 6:12 we are told: "For we wrestle not against flesh and blood, but against principalities, against powers, against the rulers of the darkness of this world, against spiritual wickedness in high places". The truth is, the world, or world system is being controlled by the devil. Scriptures states it, and our society confirms it. The world will try to conform us to its way of thinking, hence become successful in conforming us to its patterns and actions. The evil one is very subtle. We are so gently being persuaded, to accept things that are contrary to scriptures because the world accepts them, and we continue the downward slide. Things that once made us cringe, now are simply a sideshow. Remember, in the Old Testament, the Lord always commanded the Israelites to destroy everything and everyone they encountered from the land He gave them to take over. He warned King Solomon to stay from the women of the foreigners, because they would turn his heart from Him – the true and living God – to their false god. Solomon did not heed and we can read in scriptures, the consequence. The foreign women did indeed turn his heart, from our Commander-in-Chief. God knows the danger. We are to heed the warning, and make provisions to combat these dangers. I think we are at a time when a TV is not a good thing for the household of a believer that truly seeks to raise his family and himself in the fear and admonition of the Lord. It is subtly pumping, for the most part, evil into the thoughts and hearts of God's people. This is just my opinion. You will have to make the decision for yourself and family.

The danger is that, though believers are given the new (Divine) nature at conversion, we also still posses the old (fallen) nature, hence the battle that the Apostle Paul describes in the epistles. The problem is: the unbeliever has the old nature, but does not share the divine nature. In other words, we can identify with, and be affected by their old nature, but they cannot identify with our divine nature. If the believer is not filled with and walking in the spirit, as the Bible commands, he or she is susceptible to subtly being led towards gratifying the old nature by the words or actions of the unbeliever. We are to deal with unbelievers on our turf, not theirs. I am sure you can see the danger. The good thing is that, greater is He that is within us than he that is in the world. Glory to the spotless Lamb of God! We believers are to "reckon" ourselves dead to sin, as the scripture commands. We are told, in scriptures, that we do not have to obey our old nature anymore, and by God's grace and the believer yielding to the spirit, we can become, and indeed are, more than conquerors. Glory to God! Hallelujah! The reality is, as was already intimated, if we are not being transformed into the image of Christ by the Word of God, we are more than likely, subtly, being conformed to the world and its pattern of thinking.

Chapter #12

Discipline Of Believers – STEWARDSHIP

God had given us everything we have. The Bible calls them graces. Our Commander-in-Chief calls for us to be good Stewards. We were blessed with the aptitude to appreciate and appropriate these graces for the glory of God, and for the good of mankind. We are also told to work, so that we will have to help those in need. We are actually told to do our duties and obey all authorities and laws, as unto the Lord Himself (1st Peter 2:13-16). Wives are told: Submit yourselves unto your husband (Ephesians 5:22). We are bound to obey all authority that are placed over us, "as unto the Lord", except where that authority would cause us to disobey God's Word, the Bible. We have become a generation of the "instant". We seek to have everything instantly – now. Many do not wish to work hard, save and wait, for what they desire. The scriptures say, "From the sweat of your brows you shall eat bread" (Genesis 3:19). Hard work has never killed anyone. On the contrary, hard work builds character, appreciation, contentment, and many other Godly traits our Commander-in-Chief desires us to have. One of the best things we can do for our children is to teach them hard work at an early age.

The world teaches and promises instant everything – gratification, wealth, success. It was not designed that way. Today, individuals are willing to do literally anything for money. The Bible says: "For the love of money is the root of all evil" (I Timothy 6:10). Two of the most startling bumper stickers I've seen are: "Get rich or die trying", and "He who dies with the most toys wins." How alarming. This is the mindset that is leading our youths into all types of illegal activities, in the quest to "get rich", despite the means or consequence. Heaven help us! The unending quest for material things condones and nurtures this type of mindset and behavior. The individuals with earthly wealth, mind you, no matter how they've acquired it, are elevated, and placed on pedestals – in many cases idolized – in many of today's societies. Well, the Bible teaches that it does matter how we've acquired; it is just as important as, or even more important than, what we have. It's not that you got to the top that matters in God's economy; it's how you got there. Did you pull anyone down to get up? Did you compromise, lie, cheat or steal? Did you take advantage of anyone? These are the questions we ask in God's economy. We should elevate and emulate those in society that are of good moral character. King David; in Psalm 15 laments: "Lord, who shall abide in Thy tabernacle? Who shall dwell in Thy holy hill? He that walketh uprightly, and worketh righteousness, and speaketh the truth in his heart. He that backbites not with his tongue, or doeth evil to his neighbor, nor taketh up a reproach against his neighbor. In whose eyes a vile person is contemned, but he honoreth them that fear the Lord. He that sweareth to his own hurt and changeth not. He that putteth not out his money to usury, nor taketh reward against the innocent. He that doeth these things shall never be moved." Notice! One who sweareth to his own hurt and changeth not – literally, one who gives his word and keeps it, even though the circumstances have changed, and it becomes difficult for him to honor his word. There was a time when a person's word was his bond. Today, for the most part, we make promises out of our mouths that we have no intention of honoring. Our word is all that we have. If a person cannot trust our word, then we cannot be trusted – plain and simple. This is the type of individual we should be looking up to and exemplifying in our societies – persons of conviction and compassion; in a word – integrity.

If we follow the golden rule of treating others as we would like to be treated, loving our neighbors as ourselves, and, doing everything as unto the Lord, we would make some of the best workers, bosses, husbands, wives and citizens of our societies; and of most importance, be more effective purveyors of the Gospel of our the Lord Jesus Christ. A newspaper published the following in response to workers complaint about pay raises: "Many workers complain that they are paid inadequately, but they fail to factor in how much they cost the companies for which they work. Few people pay attention to the amount of time employees spend on the phone, making personal phone calls, and how the seconds turn into minutes, or how the minutes turn into hours, or how the hours translate into thousands of dollars. Some employees surf the internet at will, on the employer's time. Others print reams and reams of documents, their kid's homework, even, without thinking about the cost to the business. Employees expect the boss to give them time off to attend funerals, graduations, and weddings and appointments, all of which translate into lost time and money; but if the boss asks them to stay 15 minutes past knock-off time, they expect compensation. Mobile phones are abused, and some people use the petrol they get to do their employer's bidding to make personal runs. Some workers think little of their importance in the company and how performing at their optimum can help to secure the continued viability of their employer. For some, insubordination is their rule of thumb. Others are negligent, discourteous, wasteful and habitually absent or late." Think about it, if your boss came to your home, how many pens, papers, cups, and other trinkets, from the workplace, would he find in your dwelling. In a word, it is called stealing. Others work effectively only when the boss is around, clearly stealing the boss' time. In scriptures we are told to do our work, not as unto men, with eye service, but as unto the Lord. Believers, remember, you are doing what you do for the Lord, and unto the Lord. He is watching always; and you wish to please him and bring honor and glory to His name.

Good Stewards – Decision Making

Making decisions that are in conformity to God's will is paramount to the believer's growth. When making decisions, the first considerations should be: Will it bring glory to God? Is it good for my brother and fellow man? Consequence to self should be least considered. The questions most asked are questions like: What is in it for me? Will it make me feel/look good? All that we have belongs to God, to be used for His glory: Our time, our money our talents – our very being. We are called to be good stewards. Robert Raines writes: "Let not success make me arrogant but rather grateful and humble. Let not failure make me fearful, but rather wiser; pain or malice make be bitter but enlarge my capacity to endure and overcome, keep me vulnerable to others and so to you. Bill Marriott, in his poem, penned: "The six most important words are: "I admit that I was wrong", the five most: "You did a great job", the four most: "What do you think" the three most: "I am sorry", the two most: "Thank you", the one most important word is: "we", and the least important word is: "I". If we cannot be trusted in small matters; we will not be trusted in big ones. Often cheating begins in small almost innocent ways. An exaggerated story, an excuse that simply isn't true, an inaccurate tax form, claiming sickness as a cover up for taking the day off, skimming a few dollars off monies you are entrusted with. We call them little white lies, and then the small ones – so called – grow into more serious violations of trust. We cut corners by cheating on others, and in the end we cheat ourselves. Honesty and trust are essential in everything we do as believers – in our family life, marriage, relationships, between friends, at work and our public life. If we tell the truth we only need to tell it once. The world says there are no moral absolutes – whatever makes you feel good. The Bible says do good and it will make you feel good (Romans 12:21). God's standard is absolute. When it comes to truth, perception is as good as reality. We should never put ourselves in positions where we would even remotely appear to be dishonest, or to be doing evil. Remember, the scriptures say, shun the very appearance of wrongdoing (evil).

Good Stewards – Finance Management

Another critical area of discipline is the area of finance, and how we manage our money. We are told that 10% percent of our earnings belong to God, but we are still responsible to give offerings above and beyond, as the Holy Spirit leads. We are to pray and ask God to show us where there are areas of need, where we can contribute. The Bible says where your treasure is there will your heart be also. A big problem is we are simply not managing our finances correctly. In our day of rampant materialism, we are tempted and seduced to have what our neighbors have. We literally spend what we don't have trying to "keep up with the Jonses." When we become financially challenged – because that is what will happen eventually – we are more susceptible to give into the flesh and its desires, and fail the Lord. We need to Budget ourselves. It may seem academic; but if you only make three hundred dollars a week, budget for that amount, and stick to it. It is not that we make too little, it is just that we are spending, and living, above our means. If we made more money we would spend more and would be, basically, in the same position of always needing more. As believers, we need to be contented and faithful with what the Lord has provided. The scripture says godliness with contentment is great gain. You are to give the Lord what belongs to Him whether it is tithes, our time or our abilities; and you will see that you will always have too much. If you are a contented person, you will always have too much. If you are not a contented person, no matter how much you have, you will never have enough.

Good Stewards – Discipleship

Discipleship is another important discipline. We are told in the book of Matthew to, go ye into every nation and make disciples. We are not to look for results in evangelism. Just be obedient to the Word and tell others about Christ. The Lord will do His work. The Bible says: One plants and another waters, but God gives the increase (I Corinthians 3:6, 7). We are promised that His Word will not return void (Isaiah 55:11). We don't share Christ with people for self exaltation or immediate results, but as obedient servants, knowing that we are simply instruments of the master. God will do His work. We plant the seed of the Word; the Lord sends someone else to water with the Word, then eventually he gives the increase; and voila – the person is saved. In this manner God gets the credit – our Commander-in-Chief, the Lord Jesus Christ – and there can be no boasting on our parts. Our God is a jealous God. Humans like to take credit for God's work, but in this regard, there is no opportunity for boasting, on our part. If we truly believe what the Bible says, then people are dying and going to a Christ-less eternity every day. That includes our family members, friends, and acquaintances – everyone who dies without trusting Christ as their savior. We know they don't have to go to hell. We need to have compassion for souls. Charles Spurgeon summed it up nicely when he penned: "If a sinner will be damned, at least let them leap to hell over our bodies. And if they will perish let them perish with our arms about their knees, imploring them to stay. If hell must be filled, at least let it be filled in the teeth of our exertions, and let not one go there unwarned and un-prayed for." An unknown author also summed it up nicely, when he penned "I know inside that the flesh would like more training… but those generations passing away at the moment! They must hear of the savior! How can we wait? O Lord of the harvest, do send forth laborers! Here I am, lord. Behold me, send me. How deaf must be the deafness of the ear which has never heard the story; How blind the eye that has not looked on Christ for light; How pressed the soul that has no hope of glory; How hideous the fate of the man who knoweth only the night! God arouse us to care, to feel as He Himself does for their welfare."

The test, as believers, is not so much what we do, and would for our children and family, though very important; that is academic. The Bible says even unbelievers are good to people that are good to them. Think of those who do well for a stranger's family or even one's very enemy's family. There was a story told on a popular news program, about a drug lord. He literally reigned terror, by killing the judges and their families, to further his cause, and drug empire. Literally anyone that opposed him was killed. The authorities, in their efforts to arrest him, realized that he loved his family so much, that he was willing to risk getting caught to keep in touch with them. So the authorities kept around the clock vigils on his family, hoping that his love for them would lead him to be careless, which in turn would aid them in capturing him. Lo and behold! He was eventually cornered and killed by the authorities, while trying to keep in touch with, and protect his children. The epitaph at this man's funeral was: The man who had no care for other's children, died because he cared for his. Don't get me wrong, we are to love our families. But we are to show the same love, and be willing to sacrifice for, every one of God's creatures. We are to love the unloved, the unlovely, as our Commander-in-Chief would. If we knew there was a bomb in a building, we would warn everyone, vehemently, even to the point to forcing them out, against their will, if needs be. Well, people are dying, daily, and going to a Christ-less eternity.

The hymn writer rightly pens:

"You preach about a burning hell, you say that men will die. But if I ask you would you tell?
Why are your eyes so dry, why are your eyes so dry, why are your eyes so dry?
You claim to know the risen Christ, you say He's living still. But if I ask you would you tell?
Why are your lips so still? Why are your lips so still? Why are your lips so still?
You teach a class in Sunday school, you're doing well, you're told, you're very good at keeping rules.
Why is your heart so cold? Why is your heart so cold? Why is your heart so cold?
You sing, "Blest be the tide that binds, you sing Amazing Grace". What will you sing on judgment day? When we see Jesus' face, when we see Jesus' face, when we see Jesus' face.
The living God with eyes of tears has sent His son to die, "He said to go and tell the world",
but you won't even try, no you don't even try, no you won't even try.
Now you talk about a burning hell, you say that men will die, but if I ask you, would you tell?
Why are your eyes so dry? Why is your heart so cold? Why are your lips so still? And you won't even try? Why are your eyes so dry?"

Ask the Lord to open doors of opportunity to preach the gospel. The Bible says, how beautiful are the feet of them that preach the gospel, and then tells us: What door God opens, no man can shut. Ask God, and seek opportunities to present the gospel. Acts like offering assistance to a stranger in need may be the catalyst our Commander-in-Chief uses to open the door for a presentation of the gospel that ends up leading someone into the Army of the Lord. II Corinthians 1:4-6 says, "Who comforteth us in all our tribulation, that we may be able to comfort them which are in any trouble, by the comfort wherewith we ourselves are comforted of God….And whether we be afflicted, it is for your consolation and salvation". God comforts us to make us comforters, not to make us comfortable, for the Lord is more concerned with our character than our comfort. Notice that Paul said to the believers in II Corinthians 7:6, God comforted him with the coming of Titus. He says, "Nevertheless God, that comforteth those that are cast down, comforted us by the coming of Titus; and not by his coming only, but by the consolation wherewith he was comforted in you".

Good Steward – Modesty in dress

Another critical area of discipline is in the area of dress. Though we have liberty in Christ, we should be very careful of what we wear. Men and women are attracted and affected by what we see. We are told in scriptures not to use our liberty as license. Though we have liberty in Christ, there are guidelines and principles, found in the Bible, governing every aspect of the believer's life. When we go over those boundaries we are clearing sinning against a holy God, no doubt. The Bible says, what is not of faith is sin. The Bible tells us not to use our liberty as license to cause our brother or sister to stumble. You might be leading your brother or sister into temptation, and in some instances, outright provocation. The apostle Paul said that if his freedom to do as he pleases in doubtful matters causes a brother or sister to stumble, then he would gladly give up that freedom. He said, "I have become all things to all men, so I might win some." The words of a popular hymn sums it up well: "I gave my life for thee, my precious blood I shed, that thou might ransomed be and quickened from the dead. I gave, I gave my life for thee – what hast thou given for me. My Father's house of light, my glory circled throne, I left for earthly night, for wanderings sad and lone; I left, I left it all for thee – hast thou left aught for me. I suffered much for thee, more than thy tongue can tell, of bitterest agony, to rescue thee form hell; I've borne, I've borne it all for thee – what hast thou borne for me? And I have brought to thee, down from my home above, salvation full and free, my pardon and my love; I bring, I bring rich gifts to thee – what hast thou brought to me." Brothers and sisters, I beg of you, I implore you, for the master's name sake, please dress properly. On a personal note: Sisters, if you do not dress properly, you may cause this author, a weak brother, to stumble.

Chapter #13

Discipline Of Believers – SILENCE, SOLITUDE AND REFLECTION

Major decisions of far reaching consequence should never be made in a hurry. You are to seek God's will in much prayer, meditation upon His Word, and much introspection, considering your motives. In Proverbs 3:5,6 we are told: "Trust in the Lord with all thine heart and lean not onto thine own understanding, in all thy ways acknowledge Him and He shall direct thy paths." When you are absolutely convinced, based on the principles laid down in scriptures, and affirmed with conviction in your spirit that it is the will of God, only then do you make a final decision. In Philippians 4:6-7, we are told, "Be careful for nothing, but in all things by prayer and supplication with thanksgiving, let your request be made known unto God and the peace of God which passeth all understanding shall keep your hearts and mind through Christ Jesus."

Favorable or seemingly profitable outcomes should never be the deciding factor in deciding God's will. The most important questions asked should be: Will it bring glory to God's name? Will it further the kingdom of God? Will it benefit my spiritual growth? Or will benefit my fellow man? When you have followed what the scripture says in the area of decision making, and in much prayer and scripture meditation sought God's will, and if everything conforms to scripture and you have the peace of God about it, only then do you make a final decision. The Holy Spirit lives in the believer; therefore confirmation should be more of an inner conviction. When assured a decision is in accordance with master's perfect will, we are to make the decision and live with the consequence.

A compelling story, of a missionary named Jim Elliot, is told: Jim and his team wanted to get the gospel to a group of Indians in the middle of the jungles of South America. They readied themselves through much preparation, labor and prayer, until, eventually, they felt the Lord impressed upon them that it was the right time to make contact with the Indians. They embarked on their journey for the master, but when they landed the Indians killed them all. It may have seemed that they made a mistake. Eventually, Jim Elliott's wife went in to meet the very same Indians, to get the gospel to them. In her words she said: "My husband thought these people were important enough to give his life for, so they must be special." She went in, and due to her labor, today a vibrant Christian community exists in that area that was once inhabited by savage cannibals. Not only that, every time the story is told, I am sure it inspires many, including this author, to deeper service and devotion to the Lord. I personally recommend both movies of these faithful servants' lives. One is called, "On Wings of Splendor", and the other is called, "The End of the Spear." The Lord probably accomplished more with Jim Elliott's death, than he possibly would have ever accomplished, with his life. Ironically, Jim Elliott is the author of this famous quote: "He is no fool, who gives up what he cannot keep, for what he cannot lose." Jim Elliott did indeed give up what could not keep, to enter into that which he could never lose. This author was even more inspired when it was told that Jim and the other missionaries were in possession of guns, but had decided before, they would not use the guns to protect themselves. The reason, in their own words: "We are ready for heaven, but the savage Indians are not." Then, even more inspiring, we are later told by the one surviving attacker, who is now a Christian, that Jim and the missionaries actually raised their guns and fired one shot in the air, then lowered their guns and literally allowed the Indians to attack them. Glory to our Lord and Savior Jesus Christ who put it in the hearts of his servants to make such a sacrifice. Glory to God indeed!

To be successful you must have a plan, and a goal to accomplish that plan. Think of building a house. An Architect plans and designs, then the builder simply walks through the plan, and builds the house. As soldiers in the army of the Lord, we are to have our goals clearly defined. The goal of all believers should be to bring honor and glory to the master's name. We need to analyze our strengths and weaknesses and make provision to utilize our strengths and combat our weaknesses. We also need to periodically make analysis as to our progress. In business it is called a SWAT analysis. In businesses periodic checks are made to see if the business is making a profit. If it is not, steps are taken to arrest and counter-act the problem. In some cases drastic measures are recommended and undertaken. In likely manner, as Christians we need to analyze our progress and make adjustments where necessary. The experts say that busyness is archenemy of spirituality. Why is that so? Because it leaves you little time to plan, reflect on, and analyze the most important things in life – eternity and spiritual matters. Take time to plan, set goals, reflect on your progress. We are never to do things spontaneously. Every hour of the day, of every week, of every year, should be planned and accounted for.

Goal setting involves both our long term goals and immediate objectives. In two words – Time management. Blaze Pascal said: "our imagination is so powerful that it magnifies time, by continued reflection upon it, and so diminishes eternity, for want of reflection upon it, that we make nothing of eternity, and eternity of nothing." Notice, nowhere in the scripture are told to take ourselves out of the world permanently to serve him better, as some do. We are told to be in the world but not of the world. We are simply to be different – authentic. When the world looks at us, they will want to know what gives us the faith, courage and strength to live above its dirt and grime; thus presenting the opportunity to tell them about the one who can truly lift them out of their circumstances, and the degradation, of the filth of this wicked, fallen world. Our Commander-in-Chief – the Lord Jesus Christ deserves no less. There is a difference between quiet time with the Lord for prayer, worship and supplications; and quiet time to reflect, contemplate, and make evaluations. In the former, you are communicating with God, and in the latter you are letting God speak to you. The Bible says, "Be still and know that I am God."

Chapter #14

Discipline Of Believers – TRAINING OF THE LORD - To Build your faith or break your will.

Hebrews 12 5-11 states: "Now no chastisement for the present seemeth to be joyous, but grievous; nevertheless afterward it yieldeth the peaceable fruit of righteousness unto them which are exercised thereby."

In the book of John we are told, "These things are written that you may know", and we are also told in scriptures that the Holy Spirit bears witness with our spirit that we are children of God. We are also told in the epistles, the world will know that we are God's disciples, by our love one to another. The Bible teaches that you will know you are saved. If you met the president of the United States, no one would be able to tell you differently. If you have met the creator of the universe, you will know, that you know, that you know Him. Don't get me wrong.

Christian Soldiers

There may be times when one doubt's one's salvation – not that we should – especially at times when plagued by a besetting sin. Also, doubt is not the absence of faith, but we exercise faith in spite of our doubt. Once you've truly trusted Christ as your savior, as is laid down in Romans 9:9, 10, the assurance of your salvation should be settled. You are now free to grow in the knowledge and grace of God, as He prunes, chastises and takes you through the refining fire, to make you a better servant. God is at all times either building our faith or breaking our will. The goal is to make us Christ-like. In order to become Christ-like, we must obey the Lord and His Word. In order to obey Him, we have to trust Him. In order to trust Him, we have to know Him. In order to know him, we have to listen to Him; in order to listen to Him, we have to be close to him. In order to be close to Him, we have to spend time with him and continue to communicate with him. If we are close to the Lord as we should be, we will then see the truth, as the scriptures say: "I can do all things through Christ which strengtheneth me."

In Scriptures we are told: "Work out our salvation with fear and trembling." If you are truly born again, or born of the spirit anew, you have been made alive spiritually. The desire to do right is in you, in the form of the Holy Spirit. Notice, the scriptures remind us: "For it is God who worketh in you to do of His good pleasure." We can see that God has worked in us a new heart, at salvation, and given us His Spirit to indwell us. As the scripture says, He has quickened us alive by His Spirit. The Bible says the Holy Spirit that indwells the believer bears witness with our spirit that we are children of God. Glory to God! What blessed assurance indeed! If we are truly born again, the desire to do right and please God is within us – not a selfish desire to do right, outwardly, so that men would see and praise us, but a true desire to follow and obey God's commands and do right, simply because we love Him. Though, at times it does not always work out that way, the true desire is there, for the believer. The Apostle Paul penned it like this: "We see another law in our members." The old nature is right there to tempt us to do wrong, but glory to God, He can rescue from this body of flesh, indeed!

We are told that the world will know we are His disciples by our love one to another. If you are looking for a sign to prove one is a born anew of the spirit indeed, the true hallmark is Love. Not an <u>if love</u> or a <u>because love</u> (selfish love): Because she makes me feel good. Because I receive favors from her. Because she loves me. That is not the love the Bible describes. The love that the Bible describes is the love that shines, and shows the reality of the new birth. That is the Love of God – that selfless, sacrificial love. (An <u>in spite of love</u>). That love that would inspire one to lay down one's very life for an enemy, if needs be. That love that puts God first, others second and ourselves last. That love that is not puffed up, that love that esteems others better than ourselves. That love that loves the unlovely and the unlovable, and is willing to accept being wronged, even when right. That love that only comes from the author of Love, our Lord and Savior Jesus Christ. That love that looks down and sees a wicked sinner like Winston and says, I must go through these sufferings for Winston needs to be saved, and though I would like this cup to pass from me, not my will but Thine be done, Father. This love is not in of ourselves, for we are selfish by fallen nature. This Love is shed abroad in our hearts at the new birth. LOVE – Love Our Very Enemy. It is easy for us to love someone that is beautiful, or someone that is kind, or someone that is in a position to assist or reward us in the future. The God-love, or God kind of love, loves the ugly, the mean, the obnoxious, the dirty and filthy looking, the outcasts, people that you will never receive earthly rewards from. That is the love Jesus describes.

The experts tell us that habitual well being is disadvantageous to a species. Simply put: it's not good if things went smoothly and easily for us, all the time. If we didn't have to work, struggle at times, and stumble at times, we would first of all eat or pleasure ourselves to death, and we would not learn and grow as the master desires. In his book, The Feeling Good Hand Book, Dr. Burns states: "It is our shortcomings and not our successes that give us the opportunity for genuine caring." In the study of Church History we see that initially, Christianity was illegal and outlawed, and was persecuted vehemently throughout the Roman Empire. Believers had to meet secretly in caves, and those that were caught may have had to give their lives or renounce Christ. During, and because of the persecutions, a vibrant church was established throughout the empire. Church History also tells us that when the persecution ended, the church lost its power and became worldly and formal. We see this in the West, where, for the most part, there is religious liberty; most of our churches are worldly and formal. Compare that to the churches in countries where there is no religious freedom – places like China and many Islamic states. We hear and read of vibrant churches, with powerful testimonies.

In the lukewarm church mentioned in the book of Revelation, we see that the church is lukewarm because everything is going well. And the Lord intimates: "there would be nothing like some persecution to get them in order." Some of the most vibrant Christians today are the ones that are experiencing trials and tribulations of some sort, whether due to physical constraints, impediment or persecution in some form. Simply put, they are in positions where they have to depend on the master totally: minute by minute, hour by hour, day by day, week by week, month by month and year by year. The saying rings true: When we find out that Jesus is all we have, we will find out that He is all we need. This author recalls an experience during the Lord's ministry to shut-ins, where I was the instrument. I was used by the Lord to minister to shut-ins, to meet their spiritual and material needs, as the Lord led and provided. I can recall an elderly lady in particular that had a definite impact on me. She lived by herself and had no relative to visit or comfort her. I recall that whenever I went to encourage and minister to her, I was always surprised by the testimony, faith and love for the Lord Jesus Christ, this lady exhibited. She exhibited such steadfastness in her faith towards Christ that I always left her presence being encouraged in the faith. I also felt guilty at times; because this lady, who was in a position where she should be bitter and murmuring, actually exhibited more faith than me, at times. Why is this so? Because she is in a position where she has to depend on the master every minute of the day. She has very few earthly companions and encouragements.

Jesus said, I am the vine, ye are the branches, and unless you abide in me you cannot bear fruit (John 15:1), and apart from me you can do nothing. Remember, fruits do not simply appear. A seed has to be planted, watered and nourished. We are more prone to seek and depend on the master the way we should when we are at our wits end. We see another paradox and God's wisdom in simplicity, which confounds the wisdom of man, in the paradox of weakness to strength. The apostle Paul says: when he is weak then he is strong; therefore he will glory in his weakness. God in His infinite wisdom, and knowledge that we are prone to take credit – which I call the Lucifer syndrome – when He alone deserves all credit – has allowed this struggle, in believers, with the world, with the flesh, and with the devil. God is omnipotent (all powerful) and can do all things. God could have ordained that all believers would receive perfect bodies the instant we are born again. This would have eliminated the struggle with the fallen nature. We would no longer have the potential to sin; for the old nature would be done away with, absolutely. But, the reality is that God would never get any praise, honor or glory from the lips of these now perfect men. Can you imagine a bunch of perfect believers walking around in a world, amongst imperfect unbelievers? Every word that came out of our mouth would be close to Lucifer's words: I will, I did, I, I, I. God, in His infinite wisdom has allowed this struggle in the flesh so that He gets all the glory and praise and rightly so, for He alone deserves all honor, glory and praise.

II Corinthians 4:7 says "But we have this treasure in earthen vessels, that the excellency of the power may be of God and not of us". God gets the glory. Glory Hallelujah! The scripture also says, "For ye see your calling, brethren, how that not many wise men after the flesh, not many mighty, not many noble, are called…that no flesh should glory in His presence" (I Corinthians 1:26-29). Again God gets the glory. God said he chooses the weak things of this world to confound the wise. The world says, show me your ability – strength – and I will show where you will be best able to serve. God says show me your inability – weakness – and I will show you where I can, and will, most powerfully use you, for my honor and my glory. When we realize our inability and God's ability then he can use us. We are more apt to depend on God in the areas that we are weak, than our so called strong areas. The reality is, either way, God gives us the strength and ability. The scripture says, "In Him we live and breathe and have our being" (Acts 17:25, 28). It is simply a matter of acknowledgment. God is sometimes not as effective when using us in those areas of so-called strength, because: Number one: We think it is our strength, and we are tempted to take the credit for the success. Number two: We will be doing it in the flesh, in most cases. When we are laboring in our weak areas, we know that we have to depend on the master; so we go to him the way we should, and when His power is magnified and multiplied in and through us, we rightly give Him the praise and glory. As the scripture says, "where is boasting." When God said no flesh shall glory in His sight, He meant it.

If you recall; the devil is a created being who literally, through self delusion, thought he could steal God's glory, (even thought he could not) and take His position. Why? Because God make him perfect and beautiful, and more than likely, well endowed to carry out the task he was created for. A book I recommend reading, which addresses this topic well, is called: The Hidden Price of Greatness, by Ray Beeson and Ranabla Mack Hunsicker. This book reminds us of the fact that many people used greatly by God were people who were weak or deficient in one area or another. Glory and praise and honor belong to God, and Him alone. Glory Hallelujah. A brother in Christ, who is also a teacher, gets rave reviews for his teaching ability. He is also accredited as being one of the best in his field, by many. He accounts, "the secret to his success", in this manner: He recalls that at an early age, public speaking was a nightmare to him. The mere thought of going in front a crowd literally made him go into cold sweats. He claims that even today he has that problem, but you would never know it when you see him in front of a crowd. The secret is, he says, due to his paranoia of failing, he prays vehemently, and studies his material meticulously. In this manner, he assures himself that he would do well. Well, you see, in the process of praying, preparing meticulously, the brother becomes better equipped, thereby doing a better job than someone who does not have a problem in the public speaking arena. The brother says he always thanks the Lord, after every public speaking session, for giving him success. Do you think a brother that has more ability and confidence in this area, thanks God when he is finished speaking? No! He more than likely sounds like the wicked one, Lucifer himself: I did a great Job. Oh the riches and the Glory of God. "Where is boasting? By what man? To God be the Glory. For He alone is worthy to receive all honor, all glory and all praise.

So, we see the "secret to his success" is actually the secret to the master's success through him. Remember when Peter spoke boldly, they took note that this unlearned man, speaking with such wisdom, and boldness, who, just a little while after Jesus was crucified, not only denied him three times, but ran and hid like a coward – was with Jesus. They remembered that he was with Jesus, the true source of his strength. The apostle Paul said that he is pressured so that he will learn not to depend on himself, but on God. The reality is, it is only a matter of acknowledging the truth, for, weather we acknowledge it or not, God deserves all the credit, because without him we can do nothing, and in him we live and breathe. The following poem describes the attitude of the clay, as a potter shapes and molds it for the mastery:

"The Process"

"Sometimes I don't enjoy the pressure,
the squeezing, the going around
the wheel one more time, as you smooth out
each bump, and mould and shape me.
But I know with each turn, as I
yield to your skillful hands,
you are transferring me from crude
clay to a vessel of honor."

God disciplines or trains His children. The scripture is clear that, Whom He loves He chastises. If you are without discipline you are not a son; you are not in the kingdom. God's tries, or disciplines us, to build our faith or break our will. The devil tries us to make us fail. The Bible tells us, without faith it is impossible to please God, and that the trial of our faith is more precious than gold. Faith is synonymous with trust. God wants us to trust Him, for the more we trust Him, the more we will obey, and the more we obey the more we will become Christ-like and be effective soldiers in the army of the Lord. God is at all times working to build our faith. The Holy Spirit is constantly convicting us of sins and righteousness, but God disciplines us when we continue in disobedience. When we sin, we sin against a Holy God; we miss the mark. There is a need for an almost minute by minute check of our thoughts, motives, words and actions, and a constant need for cleansing as mentioned in 1 John 1:9 which states: "If we confess our sins he is faithful and just to forgive us and to cleanse us from all unrighteousness." God is at all times dealing with us in one area or another. As we heed the Holy Spirit's convictions and confess and forsake our sin, the Lord then shines his light into other areas, and as we confess and forsake, the process continues– light reveals more light – as the Lord continues to refine us. In the process we do not become sinless, but by the grace of God, we will sin less and become better persons.

We need to remain sensitive to the Holy Spirit's convictions, by confessing, repenting and forsaking of sins as soon as they are revealed to us by the Holy Spirit. If we let un-confessed sins build up, we can get to the point where our sensitivity to sin becomes less and less acute, literally, like building a wall – to the point where we do not hear the convictions of the Spirit. If this condition continues unchecked, we face the danger of subtly sliding back into the world. The experience of bodybuilding illustrates this point. Initially, when I first began to exercise, the weight bars were very hard on my hands. The more I worked out without gloves, the harder my hands became. Eventually I built up callouses in my hands to the point where the bars did not even bother me anymore. We can do that with the Holy Spirit, by not heeding His convictions and confessing our sins; before we know it we no longer hear the convictions of the Holy Spirit and end up backsliding, back in the world. A believer in this condition – we know from scriptures – is around the corner from what I call, a Jonah experience, but the scripture calls, loving discipline.

Backsliding does not take place overnight. It begins gradually. We first begin by not spending as much time in the Word of God, missing one or two services, skipping our morning devotion time with the Lord, not keeping our priorities in perspective, not keeping an eternal perspective; before we know it, we gradually slip back into the mud – the world. We are told that if you put a live frog in hot water to boil, it will jump out, instantly. But, if you put it in warm water and gradually turn up the dial, it will remain and boil to death. Remember, one of the attributes of the devil is subtlety – subtly, luring believers away from the ways of God, subtly causing us to lose our love, our first love – the master, the lover of our soul. I think, as believers, we should become very alarmed when a faithful church member slowly absences him/herself from fellowship. The minute this becomes apparent, investigations, and prayers should be given on the brother/sister's behalf; for we know the subtlety of neglect. Our Father and Commander-in-Chief tells us, he disciplines those he loves. The major theme of the book of Proverbs – written by the wisest man that ever lived – is that, one who hears and heeds correction is wise, and will only get wiser, as he continues to hear and heed instruction. Life is a learning process – learning from our mistakes, learning to forgive, and most of all, learning to trust God. The best thing our loving Father can do for us is to bring our sins into the open; for then we have to deal with them. The Scriptures say, "He that covereth his sins shall not prosper, but whosoever confesseth and forsaketh them shall have mercy." (Proverbs 2:13). One preacher said it like this: If you uncover your sins, God will cover it with His blood; but if you cover your sins, God will uncover it to your shame. In scriptures we are told, your sins will find you out.

The believer's attitude is very important during times of discipline. The times when we are tempted to murmur and quarrel with the Lord and say things like: I don't deserve this. Simply switch the argument around and say Lord, give me what I deserve. Those six words always humble this author. Whether we are being disciplined because of disobedience – to break our will, or unto obedience – to build our faith; our attitude should always be, as one author penned: "Master keep me to always have the mind of your Son when he said constantly; I must be about my Father's business, and "not my will, but Thine will be done. The means I leave up to You."

We believers are to accept the work that the master is doing in our lives. We are to believe that He knows what He is doing. We are to confirm His working in our lives and delight in his will, all as good soldiers of the Army of the Lord. John 4:1-3 tells us that He is shaping and fashioning us into his image. He is the potter, and we are the clay. Discipline should yield fruits of righteousness (Colossians

3:16, Psalm 199:11, Jeremiah 15:16 Deuteronomy 32:2). In scriptures, we are told to rejoice always; and we can truly rejoice knowing that nothing can happen to us apart from the master's will. Our very hairs are numbered, as the Lord says. Even our biggest adversary, Satan, has to get the master's permission before he can do anything to the believer, as can be seen from studying the book of Job. The question we need to ask ourselves constantly is: How big is our God. The reality is that the God we serve is so mighty that He can allow the devil and fallen angels to exercise their will; also let fallen sinful creatures, such as us, exercise our will; and still accomplish His will; for His council stands. Hallelujah! Glory to the only Lord of Lords and King of Kings – our Commander-in-Chief. In Romans 8:28 we are told that all things work together for good to them that love him, to them that are the called according to His purpose. An unknown author sums it up quite nicely when he penned these few words: "Though what has overtaken me was an attack of the enemy, by the time it reaches me, it has the Lord's permission; therefore all is well; for I know He will work it together with all of life's ills for His glory and my good." We can see, as an example, Moses' response to how God dealt with him in Deuteronomy 3:25, 26. Moses persistently pleaded with God to spare his life and let him see the promised land. Eventually God simply informed Moses that He will hear no more on that subject. Moses spoke no more on the subject. He simply accepted God's decision and will. Eli was informed, by God, that his sons would die, due to their disobedience. His response was simply, if it is the Lord's will, then let it be done. In the scriptures we are told that no discipline seems pleasurable, but after it yields the fruits of righteousness. King David said that he was glad that he was afflicted, for he can now teach transgressors God's ways.

The Discipline of – Church Discipline

The scripture teaches Church Discipline. This author, being a product of Church discipline, can attest to its importance. It is said that the church is the only army that abandons its wounded. That is looking at it from a human perspective. The reality is that we are in the world and not of the world. We are also told not to conform to this world. Church members have to be held to a higher standard, than non-members. Church leaders, especially, have to be held to an even higher standard. The Word of God lays down the proper protocol and attitude for church discipline. We are told: If a brother or sister persists in open un-repented sins, we are to speak to the sinning brother/sister in a spirit of meekness and love – for you can fall into that very same sin. If he/she persists in un-repented sin, we are to take two members of the church, and again, speak to the wayward brother, in a spirit of meekness and love. If the member remains un-repentant, we are to take it to the church for disciplinary action. The church hears the evidence and decides by way of vote. The Church then decides sanctions, if any, to be taken. If the sinning brother or sister continues in their disobedience, then the church is to turn him over

Christian Soldiers

to Satan, as the scripture says: "So that the spirit will be saved." Yes, take away his membership - not abandon him, but dismiss him from the membership roll, thereby showing him the error of his ways, in love. It is meant to bring him back to the fellowship, not drive him deeper into the world. We need to keep that in mind. If he is truly a brother, the Lord will bring him back. The Lord can use any stage of this process to get the disobedient brother or sister's attention. Notice, I did not say, stop him from attending the church. Nowhere in scripture are we told to stop a brother from attending church service. The Church is where he belongs. By encouraging a wayward brother or sister to find another church, we are literally abandoning him/her. The scriptural and brotherly thing to do is to encourage him/her to keep attending the same church, unless of course, his or her presence in the service would hinder a smooth and orderly flow of the service. It seems, at times, we are more concerned with what the community thinks, and how the church looks, in the eyes of men – for the master knows of our lukewarm state – than seeing our fallen brother, whom the Lord died for, restored back to fellowship. There has to be a balance, as in all things. The scripture says: If any, called a brother, persists in sin "treat him not as brother." We can still encourage that brother – while dealing with him as unto a non-member. King David said, let the wickedness of the wicked come to an end – not the wicked, but the wickedness of the wicked. We are told to love the sinner, but hate the sin – sin in anyone's life, including our own. When a professing believer backslides, it is either he was never saved, for our Commander-in-Chief says that: No one can pluck them out of my hands – or if he is saved, he is right around the corner from being broad-sided by the Lord, Jonah style. This is the truth, as laid down in scriptures. If you truly love the Lord, and He is disciplining you because of disobedience, when He is finished you will say, like David: I was glad that I was disciplined. God sent His Son to die for us, so that we could live for Him on this earth, and live with him throughout eternity. Let me make this clear: Nowhere in scriptures are believers called to martyrdom for martyrdom's sake. If we are told to disobey the Word of God, or die; then we have to do as we are told in scriptures, obey God rather than man and accept the consequence, even if it costs us our lives. Nowhere in scriptures are we told to kill ourselves or others. On the contrary, we are to be willing to give our lives, if need be, so others could live. We are to live for Him, and He will choose the time we depart this earth, and go with Him, in glory. An unknown author penned these few interesting words: "Father, If I cannot glorify you with my life, then let me glorify you unto death, just as your Son did on the cross of Calvary, when he said: 'Not my will, but Thine be done'; and in all personal attacks, let my mantra be: 'Father forgive them, for they know not what they do'. And Father, let my response be as your servant Stephen, when being stoned to death: 'Father, lay it not to their charge'" (Acts 7:60). Our mantra should eternally be: Father glorify thyself, for thou and thou alone deserve all glory. Francis of Assisi pens it better than this author ever could:

Lord, make me an instrument of your peace, Where there is hatred, let me sow love;
where there is injury, pardon; where there is doubt, faith;
where there is despair, hope; where there is darkness, light;
where there is sadness, joy;
O Divine Master, grant that I may not so much seek to be consoled as to console;
to be understood as to understand;
to be loved as to love.
For it is in giving that we receive; it is in pardoning that we are pardoned;
and it is in dying that we are born to eternal life.

Chapter #15

Discipline Of Believers
MORTIFYING "KILLING" THE FLESH

King David, though his numerous failures, was called, "a man after God's heart." One simply has to read the psalms to see that King David loved the Lord with all his heart; for when he sinned, he truly had a broken spirit and a contrite heart. David's failures truly left him broken, contrite and repentant. Don't get me wrong. God does not and cannot wink at sin. When we confess our sins, God forgives us, but we still have to live with the consequences. King David paid dearly for his sins. His child died, his children literally tore his kingdom apart, but nevertheless, God forgave him and called him a man after his own heart. The scriptures say, "The sacrifices of God are a broken spirit and a contrite heart." One pastor said he has been pastoring for over 25 years, and one of the greatest causes of apostasy – falling away – is fornication. As a sad commentary, the very same pastor has been recently been accused of sin of a sexual nature. The Bible teaches that sex is permissible only in the context of one man and one woman, in marriage. Anything outside of this is sin, and like any other sin, it is to be confessed, repented of and forsaken. Sex is a natural desire, which was ordained by God, to replenish the earth, and naturally be enjoyed. Due to man's fall, this natural desire, if not controlled and directed by the Holy Spirit, can get out of control.

The flesh is so corrupt that it will get us into all kinds of trouble. It will then die one day, and go back to the dust, leaving us to face the consequences for all eternity. When we feed our minds with the junk of the world – the lust of the eyes and the pride of life – we are literally fueling the flesh. Notice that we feed the spirit, but we fuel the flesh. Believers are not working to clean up the fallen sin nature. We are working on making the Divine nature dominant, by feeding on the Word of God, and strict discipline. This will better enable us to obey the spirit, instead of being dominated by the flesh. In I Peter 1:14, we are told, "as obedient children not fashioning yourself according to the former lust in your ignorance." The Spirit is gentle and is easily satisfied, but the flesh craves and is never satisfied. In the life of the believer, at the very moment of salvation, the battle between the flesh and Spirit begins. The fight is on at every moment. On every road, in every hallway, the god of this world is lurking, ready to devour and destroy. But, the Commander-in-Chief is also there, in the form of the Holy Spirit, within us. Glory to God that, "greater is he that is in you than he that is in the world." The victory is certain only if we let the Holy Spirit lead. When we spend time consuming worldly enticements more than the Word of God, when being amused and entertained takes precedence in our priorities over fellowship with the Father and our brothers and sisters in Christ, then our hearts begin to become cluttered, slowly and subtly drifting us away from the master. Sin begins in the heart.

The apostle Paul says: I die daily, and I bring my body in subjection. We are told to mortify – kill – the flesh. We are also told to flee from evil. There will be times when we will have to do like Joseph, and literally run. The Bible says, "The wise man foresees evil and hides himself." The experts tell us that the average male thinks about sex over 100 times during the course of a day. We are told the desire for sex, in males, is greater than the desire for food. The Bible tells us the pleasure of sin is for a season. Pleasures, and the things we look to for satisfaction – whether sex, drugs, alcohol, fame, money, power, or anything else – will never satisfy. We will always need, and want more. Notice, we fuel the flesh. King Solomon had over 1000 wives and concubines and said he tried everything to bring pleasure and satisfy his soul. At the end he penned: It is all vanity, like literally grasping at the wind – trying to catch air. We are told, by theologians, that we were created to have fellowship with God, but, due to the fall, that fellowship was broken. We were made to have our satisfaction, or to be fulfilled, in God. Everything else we try is like putting a square peg in a round hole – it will never fit. The God-shaped vacuum in us is to be filled with God, the true lover of our soul. Until Christ takes his rightful place in our hearts, we are literally grasping at the wind – literally groping in the dark, both literally and figuratively. A simple comparison between flesh and spirit can enlighten us. The flesh craves; the spirit convicts. The flesh demands; the spirit prompts. The flesh is brutal; the spirit is gentle. The flesh seeks to gratify self; the spirit seeks to glorify God. The truth is, we are to be totally dependent on God, because in reality, we are totally dependent on God – for every breath, every word, every step, literally everything. The scriptures say "for in him we breathe and have our being."

Death came to all men through one man (Romans 5:2). When Christ died, our sin nature died and was buried with him (Romans 6:3and6). That is why we are told in scriptures: "Reckon" yourself dead to sin. We are to believe and act like it; for sin no longer has dominion over us. The scripture says, but we also receive with him the resurrection to a new life (Romans 6:4). We are told, do not let sin reign in your mortal bodies to obey its evil desires (Romans 6:11). Notice, we obey evil desires. Romans 6:3, 4 tell us not to offer our members, or bodies, unto sin, but unto righteousness. The idea is: we do not have to obey evil desires any longer. Romans 6:16-19 tells us: Just as disobedience leads to sin, and sin leads to death; obedience leads to righteousness, and righteousness leads to holiness. *The senses are the avenues to our soul from the world: Feeling, seeing touching, smelling and hearing. This information, if used as a basis of our decisions, make for a carnal Christian. So we shouldn't feed our senses at all; rather we should feed our soul/spirit with information from the Word of God and make our decisions based on what the Spirit teaches us, thus making a spiritual Christian.* When Christ died, not only was our sin nature buried with Him, but we received within the resurrection to a new life in Christ Jesus (Rom 6:4). Hallelujah! Glory to God! Rom 7:6 tells us, we can now serve in the new way of the spirit, not in the old way of the written code. At salvation, the Holy Spirit circumcises us, giving freedom and liberty from the flesh and ways of the world. The believer is given a new heart, but we have to change our way of thinking. **One author said it is easier to suppress the first desire than to satisfy all the following.** The scriptures are our food and our weapon. In view of God's mercy, the least we can do, is to present our bodies a living sacrifice, as commanded in Rom 12:1, and guard our hearts with all diligence, for out of it are truly the issues of life. Evil thoughts come from an evil heart. The spirit is willing, but the flesh is truly weak. The sinful nature desires what is contrary to the spirit, for they are in conflict, but glory to God, there is victory in Christ Jesus, our savior, friend, and Commander-in-Chief.

Microsoft, the computer software giant issues a patch periodically, to fix imperfections in its operating systems. Well, our Commander-in-Chief has issued a patch – His son, the Living Word, the scriptures, the written Word, His Holy Spirit within, and a direct phone line of communication through prayer to His throne of grace 24

Christian Soldiers

hours a day and 7 days a week. The scriptures tell us, in the last days, people will have a form of godliness but deny the power therein. Every time we give in to enticements of the flesh, we are truly denying the power of God. The Bible tells us, the power that raised Christ from the dead, is available to the child of God. The reality is, Christ could come back at any moment. If we truly believe that, we ought to live like it. Anything we do, apart from what we do for the kingdom of God, is literally building castles in the sand; don't build sand castles; let us build castles in the sky.

Chapter #16

Discipline Of Believers
MOTIVATION FOR DOING RIGHT (THE LOVE OF GOD)

We are saved by Grace through faith. Salvation is a done deal in God's Economy of Eternity. We are seated in heavenly places in Christ Jesus. In man's Economy of time, our salvation is also absolute at conversion – for nothing can be added or taken away, but it is being practically appreciated and appropriated in three parts. The believer's action in no way affects his or her position in Christ. It does determine how effective we can be for the Kingdom of God, and how rewarded we will be in glory. Just as Soldiers remain focused on their mission, we are to keep our eyes on Christ Jesus, and the prize.

We were born with a free will. God does not want robots, for he could have made us absolutely obedient by nature, and that would have settled the disobedience problem. God wants us to seek him, serve and glorify him willingly, not because we fear him, but because we love him. Fear can be overcome, but love overcomes. The scripture says, perfect love casts out all fear. Fear has to do with torment. The apostle Paul said the love of God constrains him to do right. God said if you love me keep my commandments. Positionally, our righteousness is in Christ Jesus, through Christ Jesus and because of Christ Jesus. Every sin committed before salvation has been wiped away, never to be remembered or used against us, in this life or the life to come. The sins we commit after salvation, when confessed, forsaken and repented of, are wiped away, but, we will deal with the consequences at the judgment seat of Christ, unto rewards or loss. We are to live our lives to please God – not out of a legalistic obligation to the written law, but out of a heartfelt devotion to Christ Jesus our Lord and savior; for the only reason we have access to a Holy God, is because of what Christ did on the Calvary's cross. *All believers' sins are wiped away at salvation – past, present and future. None of them will ever be brought before us at any time. When Jesus died and shed His blood on the cross for the payment of sin – all of our sins were future. The Judgment Seat of Christ is not a judgment for sin; it is a judgment of our works. The cross was when sin was judged.*

Practically, our righteousness is confessing our sins (1st John 1:9). The scripture says, there is no condemnation to those who are in Christ Jesus, and that nothing can separate us from the love of God in Christ Jesus. Nothing – including our sins. The reason we sometimes think we can earn merit points, in the master's eyes, with good deeds, is because we are sometimes too far from Him. Get closer and I guarantee your bubble will be burst. It always bursts mine. You will fall down on your face, like everyone in scripture who encountered the master in his Glory, and say, away from me, for I am a sinful man. Those that are in Christ cannot be good enough to gain God's favor, nor bad enough to lose His favor. Our righteousness is like filthy rags. There is no love of God apart from the precious blood and righteousness of Jesus Christ. Apart from Christ, there is only judgment and hell fire. Positionally, we are perfectly righteous in the eyes of God. Those of us who have placed our trust in Christ have Christ's righteousness imputed to us. This is the only reason we can approach the throne of grace, boldly, as the scripture says. Notice, God said boldly – not presumptuously. Practically God deals with us as his children – favor for doing good, chastisement for doing bad. This treatment is not onto salvation, but unto sanctification, to make us Christ-like, thereby giving us the ability to accomplish our mission of glorifying God, and being effective witnesses to the gospel of His salvation. Glory Hallelujah! Jesus set me free!

The believer needs to understand that he is saved by grace alone, through faith alone – nothing added, nothing taken away. This assurance will lead you have the kind of attitude that will give you room to make mistakes, confess and forsake, get up and continue to grow in the grace of our Lord and Savior Jesus Christ. The believer should look at failures as stepping stones, not stumbling blocks. Get up and go higher in Thee, as the hymn writer says. The master knows your heart and your desire to please him. Jesus set the example by showing us that we can totally obey God, and avoid sin. Gal 5:16 tells us: "Walk in the spirit and you will not fulfill the desires of the flesh." The believer's goal is to bring honor and glory to God. Blessings are a by-product. When we extend too much time and energy on things of this life, rather than things of eternity we have missed the mark. The believer needs to, moment by moment, get an accurate picture of God's holiness, and an accurate picture of sin and the infinite distance that separates the two. This perspective will revolutionize the way we live and think. We can compare an atom to a ball the size of the entire universe, and that would not even do justice to convey the infinite distance between the absolute holiness of God and absolute sinfulness of fallen man. The power to obey is in all believers. A famous real estate commercial asks the question: what is the secret to home buying and selling? The answer given: location, location, location. And an IT instructor said that the secret to mastering the computer is practice, practice, practice. The secret to becoming Christ-like and staying Christ-like is obedience and discipline, obedience and discipline, obedience and discipline, until the master comes or calls.

Our motivation to do right, and mantra, should always be: Because I love my Savior. He died for me, and no matter if he never does anything more for me in this lifetime, he has done more than I ever deserve and can ever repay. I want to always seek to please him. A blessing is a byproduct of doing God's will. The scripture says when we've done our master's will, we are to say: I am an unprofitable servant. Our attitude should not be what can the Kingdom of God do for me? It should be what can God do for the Kingdom, through me and by extension, my fellow. We are not to, so much to seek to be blessed, but seek to be a blessing to the Lord and others. The hymn writer sings: Make me a channel of blessing oh savior I pray. The words blessing and healings are two of the most misused words among believers today. Yes! God has promised to bless us, which he already has, and does every day. The scripture reminds us: It is because of his mercies that we are not consumed. If we woke up this morning, he has blessed us. But we miss the mark when we forget that God has infinitely blessed us spiritually, by giving us eternal life and a home in heaven with him. One author rightfully penned: "When miraculous healings becomes the object of our faith, people ask, why should we suffer, but when discipleship becomes the object of our faith, we ask how can we turn our suffering to the service of our neighbors, to our spiritual growth and to the glory of God?" As we vaguely begin to apprehend and appreciate the Love of God, it will bring us to tears of Joy. Similarly, as we vaguely begin to apprehend and appreciate the Holiness of God, it will bring you to tears of sorrow, because of sin. But thanks be to God! But thanks be to God! But thanks be to God indeed! We practice spiritual disciplines to be better prepared to fight the spiritual battle, and to please our Commander-in-Chief, because we love Him, plain and simple. We should hear the master say, every waking moment, Winston if you love me, show the world by keeping my commandments and loving your brother.

Chapter #17

Duty of Believers – **OBEDIENCE**

"Dearly beloved, I beseech you as strangers and pilgrims, abstain from fleshly lusts, which war against the soul;" (1st Peter 2:11)

One needs to read the Old Testament and see how God dealt with sin (Disobedience, all sin is disobedience) before Christ came, to appreciate the reality and the horror of sin to a Holy God. God is a Holy God, and He says "Be ye Holy, for I am Holy". Christ suffered and died because of sins (Adam and Eve's and yours and mine). The world is the way it is because of sins (Adam and Eve's and yours and mine). God's chosen people, Israel, are being persecuted and attacked throughout the world due to disobedience. Make no mistake they are God's chosen people. The devil is against Israel because they are the apple of God's eyes. The Bible tells us that the gifts and calling of God are irrevocable. We are commanded to pray for the peace of Jerusalem. The Lord will deal with them as a nation in the future, though in this dispensation they must repent and be saved by grace through faith as we all must. Sin, in any form, short circuits God's love and Grace from being appreciated and appropriated in our lives, and through our lives, to its fullest; especially sexual sins. Why? The Bible says every other sin is outside the body. 1st Corinthians 6:18-20 says, "Flee fornication. Every sin that a man does is without the body, but he that commits fornication sinneth against his own body. What? Know ye not that your body is the temple of the Holy Ghost which is in you, which you have of God, and ye are not your own? For ye are bought with a price: therefore glorify God in your body and in your spirit, which are God's." When we commit sexual sins, (any sex outside the context of one man and one woman, in marriage, exclusively, and absolutely) we are literally joining the body of Christ to a harlot. 1st Corinthians 6:15 and 16 says, "Know ye not that your bodies are the members of Christ? Shall I then take the members of Christ, and make them the members of a harlot? God forbid. What? Know ye not that he which is joined to a harlot is one body? For two, saith he, shall be on flesh." Remember, every other sin is outside the body, and as the scripture says, the two shall become one. Christ is the head, and we are body; when we commit sexual sins we are literally joining Christ's body to a harlot. God is a jealous God.

Every desire we have can be fulfilled in Christ. We were meant to have our sufficiency or satisfaction in Him. Sex in its proper context, according to the Bible is: Between a married man and woman exclusively and absolutely.

A single person is to abstain from sex, absolutely and exclusively, until marriage. This would be considered sexual purity, and it can be satisfied in Christ, to the point where one is truly filled. Sexual sins – especially – short circuits God's Love from operating in our lives to its fullest. Husbands, wives and singles need to understand that, in sexual purity, you will be fully satisfied,because it will be complimented and completed by God's love in you, and complimented and completed by God's love through you. You will be satisfied fully, to never thirst again; for you will be drinking living water, from the well that never runs dry. Sing Glory to God! As the scripture says, "Drink water out of thine own cistern, and running water out of thine own well" (Proverbs 5:15). He is able, not only to save, as the song says, but he is also able to keep, and more than abundantly able to satisfy. Glory Hallelujah!

The Bible writers employed the experience of sexual intimacy as a metaphor for spiritual ecstasy. In the songs of Solomon, Chapter #2, we see that the one offering himself as the object of our love is the Rose of Sharon, the Lilly of the Valley, the bright and morning star – Christ Himself. The Church is called the bride of Christ, with Christ being the Groom. Our body is the temple of God, and God the Holy Spirit lives in us. Sexual impurity in any form violates the temple, and, as was intimated, we are literally joining the temple with a harlot – a prostitute. Sexual purity is essential in order for a believer to experience the love of Christ to its fullest. Sexual impurity in any form violates and interrupts the intimacy or spiritual ecstasy with God. When we commit sexual sins, we are limiting ourselves from experiencing God's love fully. When we commit sexual sins, we are sacrificing the eternal love of God on the altar of temporary lust of the flesh. Remember the scripture says, "the pleasures of sin are for a season." When we commit sexual sins, we minimize the possibility of experiencing that intimacy we should experience with God – the true lover of our soul – to the fullest. We are literally settling for second best! We are literally short-changing ourselves, and settling for seconds of temporary pleasure instead of resting in our first love, the eternal lover of our soul – the love of God that surpasses all understanding.

As was stated in earlier, one pastor said that in his 25 years of experience, sexual sin is one of the major causes of Christians falling away from the faith. At the printing of this book, the very same pastor, a man who probably loves the master more than I do, now stands accused of sexual sins. The very same pastor who quotes, many times in his sermons, these words: "If you uncover your sins, God will cover it with his blood; but if you cover your sins, God will uncover it to your shame." None of us are immune. Take heed lest we fall. But for the grace of God! But for the grace of God! But thanks be to God, indeed! The following article taken from Leadership Magazine, says it all. The author begins: "Driving through Wisconsin on vacation this summer, a LEADERSHIP staff member passed a huge sign in the middle of the bucolic countryside. "Naughty Things for Nice People," it proclaimed, and as if to prove it, a gigantic cuddly bear peered out from beside the words "Adult Novelties." "What's that mean, Dad?" came the question from the ten-year-old boy in the back of the station wagon. "Yeah," piped up the siblings, "what's that all about, Dad?' Such questions abound these days, as media penetrate our homes and station wagons with not just sleazy sex but carefully packaged titillations."

"One report has it that a recent convention of youth pastors created the highest rental of X-rated movies in the hotel's history. More than 80% of all customers signing up for cable TV opt for the erotic films. The availability –the near-ubiquity-of so many sexual enticements, the constant barrage of innuendoes, and the nonstop polemic for indulgence inevitably attracts. Many rationales tempt the mind of the Christian leader: 'I have to know what's going on…Voyeurism is better than adultery…I need moderation-total deprivation isn't necessary.' Admittedly, there are no easy answers. We cannot shut off either our brains or our glands. But consider the following article by a man in full-time ministry. The article is blunt. It's not the usual LEADERSHIP article. But we felt it important to be just this blunt and realistic. Sexual temptations in many forms have always lured Christians, but today's opportunities and climate make this article especially relevant to all of us." The author goes on to quote the following poem before he continues the article: "Lust is the ape that gibbers in our loins. Tame him as we will by day, he rages all the wilder in our dreams by night. Just when we think we're safe from him, he rises up his ugly head and smirks, and there's no river in the world flows cold and strong enough to strike him down. Almighty God, why dost thou deck men out with such a loathsome toy? By Frederick Buechner.

The Leadership staff member continues with the following article from an anonymous source: "I am writing this article anonymously because I am embarrassed. Embarrassed for my wife and children, yes, but embarrassed most for myself. I will tell of my personal battle with lust, and if I believed I were the only one who fought in that war, I would not waste emotional energy dredging up stained and painful memories. But I believe my experience is not uncommon, is perhaps even typical of pastors, writers and conference speakers. No one talks about it. No one writes about it. But it's there, like an unacknowledged cancer that metastasizes best when no one goes for X-rays or feels for lumps. I know I am not alone, because the few times I have opened up and shared my struggles with Christian friends, they have replied with Doppler-ganger stories of exactly the same stages of awakening, obsession, possession. Years from now, when socio-historians sift through the documents describing our times, they will undoubtedly come up with elegant explanations of why men who grew up in church homes are oversexed, and why women who grew in those same environments emerged uptight and somewhat disinterested in sex. But I leave that to future analysis." The anonymous author goes on to document his double life of sleaze and degradation in the form of pornography, strip clubs, and prostitutes, in his desire to fulfill his lustful appetites. Finally the anonymous author was delivered from this sin, by the Lord (Glory to God!), and he penned the following words. "Purity is the condition for a higher lover –for a possession superior to all possessions – GOD HIMSELF. Sins are not a list of petty irritations drawn up for the sake of a jealous God. They are, rather, a description of the impediments to spiritual growth."

"We are the ones who suffer if we sin, by forfeiting the development of character and Christ likeness that would have resulted if we had not sinned. Sin limits one's intimacy with God. The love he offers is so transcendent and possessing that it requires our faculties to be purified and cleansed before we can possible contain it; could He in fact, substitute another thirst and another hunger for the one I have never filled? Would living water somehow quench lust? That was the gamble of faith. Impurities block you from experiencing God's full love." Purity is a precondition to see God in His highest, as much as we can in this sinful body. Purity is the precondition to experience that Higher Love, the eternal Love of God – a possession superior to all possessions. Sin limits one's intimacy with God. "God's love is so transcendent and possessing that it requires our faculties to be purified and cleansed of, especially, sexual sins before we can possibly contain it. The anonymous author ends with the following words: "What I become as I highlight my

Christian Soldiers

citizenship in the kingdom of God is far more important than anything I could become if all of my fantasies were somehow fulfilled". Copyright 1982 Christianity Today International. Reprinted by permission of Leadership journal. WWW.leadershipjournal.net. Oh the matchless grace of God! Hallelujah to the Lamb! Glory Hallelujah. The scripture says, "Blessed are the pure in heart, for they shall see God."

When we believers sin continuously, without confessing to the Lord and forsaking those sins, we are putting Christ to an open shame, crucifying Him all over again, literally – just as when He was on the cross, where He was mocked, jeered, laughed at, slapped, spat upon, and ridiculed by all passersby. God sees our secret sins, and it breaks his heart. The world sees our open sins, and they also ridicule the Master. Sin begins in the heart. The scripture says in James 1:13-15, "Let no man say when he is tempted. I am tempted of God: for God cannot be tempted with evil, neither tempteth he any man: But every man is tempted when he is drawn away of his own lust and enticed. Then when lust hath conceived, it bringeth forth sin: and sin, when it is finished, bringeth forth death." And sin is progressive. Righteousness also begins in the heart. Romans 6:16 and 19 says, "Know ye not, that to whom ye yield yourselves servant to obey, his servants ye are to whom ye obey, whether of sin unto death, or of obedience unto righteousness?...I speak after the manner of men because of the infirmity of your flesh: for as ye have yielded your members servants to uncleanness and to iniquity unto iniquity; even so now yield your members servants to righteousness unto holiness". And righteousness is also progressive. Glory to the Lamb!

The story of Enron, that infamous energy company which declared bankruptcy, after being accused of many illegal activities, underscores the danger and seriousness of lying. The executives first began by embellishing their accounting numbers, then outright lying to cover it up, which eventually lead to outright fraud. The story of King David, a man after God's own heart, underscores the danger and seriousness of lusting. He began by looking at Bathsheba, then he lusted, then he committed adultery, then he murdered her husband. We have to run from sin in our hearts, first and foremost. If we let it get past our hearts, then we will have to literally run from it physically – run as though our very lives depended on it, just as Joseph did; for such is the danger and severity of sin. When you are tempted to keep looking, which will lead to lust, then to fornication; the mantra should be, always, as the famous slang goes: DON'T EVEN THINK ABOUT IT!

Transforming the mind, as Romans 12 commands, does not take place in a vacuum. We are not simply, trying not to look, or think, about things that will entice/excite our flesh. We are replacing those terrible thoughts with the Word of God. This is very important. If we do not replace these thoughts, we leave a vacuum and we end up replacing them with the same terrible thoughts, or even worse; over and over again. Luke 11:24 – 26 tells us: "When an unclean spirit goes out of a man, he goes through dry places, seeking rest; and finding none, he says I will return unto my house whence I came. And when he cometh, he findeth it swept and garnished. Then goeth he, and taketh to him seven other spirits more wicked than himself and they enter in, and dwell there and the last state of that man is worse than the first." Terrible thoughts are not demons in of themselves; though some may be initiated by demons; but the principle of not leaving a vacuum is the same. We are to obey Philippians 4:8: "Whatsoever things are true, whatsoever things are noble, whatsoever things are just, whatsoever things are pure, whatsoever things are lovely, whatsoever things are of a good report, if there is any virtue and if there is anything praiseworthy think on these things. THINK ON THESE THINGS! Oh wretched man that I am! Who shall deliver me from this body of death? Thanks be to God – through Jesus Christ our Lord! He is abundantly able. Singing glory hallelujah, Jesus set me free. Who the Son sets free is free indeed. Freedom from serving the flesh and self, to freedom to worship God! Glory to the Lamb! For He alone is worthy to receive all honor, all glory and all praise! For He alone is able!

Chapter #18

THE ULTIMATE DISCIPLINE THE CROSS

1st Corinthians 2:8 states, "Which none of the princes of this world knew: for had they known it, they would not have crucified the Lord of glory". Acts 2:23 states, "Him being delivered by the determinate counsel and foreknowledge of God, ye have taken, and by wicked hands have crucified and slain: Whom God hath raised up" They set out to do what your hand had determined to do when you allowed them to crucify Christ. 1st Corinthians 1:18 states, "For the preaching of the cross is to them that perish foolishness; but unto us which are saved it is the power of God."

What Christ went through on the Cross was the discipline of all discipline. Let us consider what the God-Man – Christ Jesus, went through for hell deserving, disobedient sinners such as you and me. This discipline was necessary for our salvation; for without it, no amount of discipline on our part would matter. For as the apostle Paul said, "If Christ did not die on the Cross for our sins, and rise from the dead; we would be of all men most pitiable." Our Lord and Savior was falsely accused, and did not open his mouth to defend himself. He was betrayed and abandoned by his contemporaries, and did not disown them, but prayed for them. He was slapped, spat upon, whipped, had a crown of thorns placed on his head, made to carry a heavy cross for miles, beaten, stabbed in the side, had nails hammered in his hands and feet and left to die a cruel death on a cross. As the hymn writer says: "He could have called ten thousand angels, to destroy the world and set Him free, but He died alone, for you and me." He did not raise a finger to defend himself. Oh the riches of His Grace and Love. He said, "Father forgive them for they know not what they do". Hallelujah, what a savior indeed! Remember, He knew in advance what He would have to go through. He said, "Father if this cup could pass from me, yet not as I will, but Thy will be done." Thy will be done indeed. This should be our cry, minute by minute, hour by hour, day by day, week by week, month by month and year by year, until the Lord comes or calls. In light of what He has endured for us, what can we not endure for him!

PART – D

<u>GLORIFICATION –</u>
Transformation to perfection
ARMY OF THE LORD VICTORIOUS

Chapter #1

Fate of Satan and fallen Angels

The Scripture teaches that Satan will be bound for one thousand years first, and then released. "And I saw an angel come down from heaven, having the key of the bottomless pit and a great chain in his hand, and he laid hold of the dragon that old serpent, which is the Devil and Satan, and bound him a thousand years, and cast him into the bottomless pit, and shut him up, and set a seal upon him, that he should deceive the nations no more, till the thousand years should be fulfilled: and after that he must be loosed a little season" (Revelation 20:2 and 3). Then his final end (V. 19:20), "and the beast was taken, and with him the false prophet that wrought miracles before him, with which he deceived them that had received the mark of the beast and them that worshipped his image. These both were cast alive into a Lake of Fire burning with brimstone." Satan and the fallen angels will go to the Lake of Fire to burn eternally. The scriptures do not tell us why God offered mankind a second chance, but there is no second chance for Satan and his angels. In this we have to accept the fact as the scripture says, "The secret things belong to the Lord our God: but those things which are revealed belong unto us and our children for ever, that we may do all the words of this law" (Deuteronomy 29:29).

Chapter #2

Fate of Non-Believers

In the story of the rich man and Lazarus, we see that the non-believer does not get a second chance, or probationary period to repent, as some teach. It is now or never. The scripture says, "And in hell he lifted up his eyes, being in torments, and seeth Abraham afar off and Lazarus in his bosom. And he cried and said, father Abraham have mercy on me, and send Lazarus, that he may dip the tip of his finger in water and cool my tongue, for I am tormented in this flame" (Luke 16:25 – 31). Non-believers are in a place of torment waiting to go to the actual Lake of Fire, with Satan and his fallen angels. We read, "And I saw the dead, small and great, stand before God; and the books were opened: and another book was opened, which is the book of life: and the dead were judged out of those things which were written in the books, according to their works, and death and hell were cast into the Lake of Fire. This is the second death. And whosoever was not found written in the book of life was cast into the Lake of Fire" (Revelation 20:15).

The sad reality is non-believers, all those who have never trusted Christ as Savior, will go to the Lake of Fire to burn eternally, with Satan and his fallen angels. The tragedy is that no human being has to go there, for Jesus paid it all. We should be shouting it in the streets, on the roof tops, in the towns, literally everywhere the wind will take our voices, for Jesus paid it all indeed. If they would only believe and be saved.

Chapter #3

Fate of Believers

Those who "die", so to speak, before the Lord comes back, will go to be with the Lord. The apostle Paul said "We are confident, I say, and willing rather to be absent from the body, and to be present with the Lord" (II Corinthians 4:8). Those who are alive at the second coming of the Lord, (which can be at any moment, for no man knoweth the day or hour) will instantly be raised with glorified bodies, and be caught up to be with the Lord in the air. The scriptures say, "In a moment, in the twinkling of an eye, at the last trump: for the trumpet shall sound, and the dead shall be raised incorruptible, and we shall be changed. For this corruptible must put on incorruption, and this mortal must put on immortality" (I Corinthians 15:52). The eventual end of all believers, after all things are fulfilled and complete, will be in the master's presence, for all eternity. Glory Hallelujah! "And I saw a new heaven and a new earth: for the first heaven and the first earth were passed away; and there was no more sea. And I saw the holy city, New Jerusalem, coming down from God out of heaven, prepared as a bride adorned for her husband. And I heard a great voice out of haven saying, behold, the tabernacle of God is with men, and he will dwell with them, and be their God. And God shall wipe away all tears from their eyes; and there shall be no more death, neither sorrow, nor crying, neither shall there be any more pain: for the former things are passed away. And he that sat upon the throne said, behold, I make all things new. And he saith unto me, it is done. I am the Alpha and Omega, the beginning and the end. I will give unto him that is athirst of the fountain of the water of life freely. He that overcometh shall inherit all things; and I will be his God, and he shall be my son" (Revelation 21:1-8). The scriptures tell us, eyes have not seen nor ear heard what is in store for those who love the Lord. Glory to His name indeed! We will be saved eternally from the presence of sin. "And God shall wipe away all tears from their eyes; and there shall be no more death, neither sorrow, nor crying, neither shall there be any more pain: for the former things are passed away. Are we going to a better place? Hallelujah, Glory and praises to the Lamb!

ABOUT THE AUTHOR

Mr. Abrams is currently a member of the Gray's Farm Fundamental Baptist Church in the Twin Island State of Antigua & Barbuda, in the West Indies. This is the first of two books he has authored, the second being "The Master's Voice – Hearing & Heeding God's Will for your Life. Please visit the following website for more information: www.anotherchanceministries.org

CPSIA information can be obtained
at www.ICGtesting.com
Printed in the USA
BVHW03s1628120218
507905BV00001B/12/P